K

Language Teaching:
A Scheme for Teacher Education

Editors: C N Candlin and H G W...

Evaluation

Pauline Rea-Dickins and
Kevin Germaine

Oxford University Press

Oxford University Press
Great Clarendon Street, Oxford OX2 6DP

Oxford New York
Auckland Bangkok Buenos Aires Cape Town Chennai
Dar es Salaam Delhi Hong Kong Istanbul Karachi Kolkata
Kuala Lumpur Madrid Melbourne Mexico City Mumbai
Nairobi São Paulo Shanghai Taipei Tokyo Toronto

OXFORD and OXFORD ENGLISH
are trade marks of Oxford University Press

ISBN 0 19 437138 7

© Oxford University Press 1992

First published 1992
Sixth impression 2003

Any websites referred to in this publication are in the public domain and
their addresses are provided by Oxford University Press for information only.
Oxford University Press disclaims any responsibility for the content.

Phototypeset by Wyvern Typesetting Ltd, Bristol

Printed in China

To James, Joseph, and Peter

Contents

Section Three: Exploring evaluation potential

The authors and series editors

Pauline Rea-Dickins is Head of the Language Testing and Evaluation Unit in the Centre for English Language Teacher Education at the University of Warwick. She has a Ph.D in testing from Lancaster University and has worked in a variety of EFL/ESL contexts world-wide. Her main research interests are in language testing and educational evaluation in ELT.

Kevin Germaine is MA Programme Director (Applied Linguistics and ELT) at St Mary's University College, Strawberry Hill, Twickenham. He lectures on the postgraduate and the undergraduate general linguistics modular degree programmes. His research interests include evaluation and management, project sustainability, and teacher education.

Henry Widdowson is Professor of English for Speakers of Other Languages at the University of London Institute of Education, and Professor of Applied Linguistics at the University of Essex. He was previously Lecturer in Applied Linguistics at the University of Edinburgh, and has also worked as an English Language Officer for the British Council in Sri Lanka and Bangladesh.

Christopher N. Candlin is Professor and Chair of Linguistics in the School of English and Linguistics at Macquarie University, Sydney, and Executive Director of the National Centre for English Language Teaching and Research, having previously been Professor of Applied Linguistics and Director of the Centre for Language in Social Life at the University of Lancaster. He also co-founded and directed the Institute for English Language Education at Lancaster.

Through work with The British Council, The Council of Europe, and other agencies, both Editors have had extensive and varied experience of language teaching, teacher education, and curriculum development overseas, and both contribute to seminars, conferences, and professional journals.

Introduction

Evaluation

The purpose of this book is to introduce language teaching professionals to the concept and practice of evaluation. We examine the nature, principles, and practice of evaluation and develop a framework that may be subsequently used by readers for their own evaluation activities. We do not limit ourselves to concerns of testing students' language abilities but present an expanded view of evaluation that may be used as a means to curriculum and teacher development.

In Section One we begin by examining the nature and parameters of evaluation in its broadest sense. We look at what evaluation is and its role in education. We then explore the relationships between evaluation and innovation, management, and context, and examine the importance of evaluation as an essential tool in the development of language teaching and learning. The remainder of the section is concerned with the different purposes for evaluation, the areas that evaluation may focus on, and the procedures that may be used in evaluating the language teaching and learning process.

Section Two closely parallels the first section. Here we present various examples of evaluations which include those of projects and courses, methodology, materials, teachers, and learner outcomes. Through a critical review of examples, the major principles of systematic evaluation are revealed. One of the main points that we emphasize is the need to evaluate what *actually* happens in classrooms, as opposed to examining what teachers *think* happens. In other words, evaluation takes us right into the classroom to describe, analyse, and interpret what actually occurs when teaching and learning take place.

The purpose of Section Three is two-fold. Firstly, we encourage readers to think about different procedures that may be used in the collection of evaluation data. We provide opportunities for the design of questionnaires, observation sheets, and questions for an interview. Secondly, readers are invited to think about and experiment with evaluations within their own language teaching and learning contexts. The focal points that we suggest include the evaluation of classroom methodology, materials, teacher, and learners.

We feel that evaluation has a very important role to play in the improvement of teaching and learning. It is something that should not be seen as an additional 'chore' for teachers. Evaluation is to be considered the *means* by which both teaching and learning may function more efficiently and quality be assured.

The aim of this book is therefore to create in the reader an awareness of the range of applications that are possible for evaluation of various aspects of the language classroom. It seeks to develop insights and skills necessary for the implementation of evaluation activities in language teaching and learning, in particular in those areas which have up to now been most neglected.

We should like to thank both our editors for their guidance in the preparation of this book. In particular, we are very grateful to our main editor, Henry Widdowson, for the great deal of assistance and insights he has provided during the writing of this book. Any shortcomings in the book are, however, ours.

Pauline Rea-Dickins
Kevin Germaine

Language Teaching:
A Scheme for Teacher Education

The purpose of this scheme of books is to engage language teachers in a process of continual professional development. We have designed it so as to guide teachers towards the critical appraisal of ideas and the informed application of these ideas in their own classrooms. The scheme provides the means for teachers to take the initiative themselves in pedagogic planning. The emphasis is on critical enquiry as a basis for effective action.

We believe that advances in language teaching stem from the independent efforts of teachers in their own classrooms. This independence is not brought about by imposing fixed ideas and promoting fashionable formulas. It can only occur where teachers, individually or collectively, explore principles and experiment with techniques. Our purpose is to offer guidance on how this might be achieved.

The scheme consists of three sub-series of books covering areas of enquiry and practice of immediate relevance to language teaching and learning. Sub-series 1 focuses on areas of *language knowledge*, with books linked to the conventional levels of linguistic description: pronunciation, vocabulary, grammar, and discourse. Sub-series 2 focuses on different *modes of behaviour* which realize this knowledge. It is concerned with the pedagogic skills of speaking, listening, reading, and writing. Sub-series 3 (of which this present volume forms a part) focuses on a variety of *modes of action* which are needed if this knowledge and behaviour is to be acquired in the operation of language teaching. The books in this sub-series have to do with such topics as syllabus design, the content of language courses, and aspects of methodology and evaluation.

This sub-division of the field is not meant to suggest that different topics can be dealt with in isolation. On the contrary, the concept of a scheme implies making coherent links between all these different areas of enquiry and activity. We wish to emphasize how their integration formalizes the complex factors present in any teaching process. Each book, then, highlights a particular topic, but also deals contingently with other issues, themselves treated as focal in other books in the series. Clearly, an enquiry into a mode of behaviour like speaking, for example, must also refer to aspects of language knowledge which it realizes. It must also connect to modes of action which can be directed at developing this behaviour in learners. As elements of the whole scheme, therefore, books cross-refer both within and across the different sub-series.

This principle of cross-reference which links the elements of the scheme is also applied to the internal design of the different interrelated books within it. Thus, each book contains three sections, which, by a combination of text and task, engage the reader in a principled enquiry into ideas and practices. The first section of each book makes explicit those theoretical ideas which bear on the topic in question. It provides a conceptual framework for those sections which follow. Here the text has a mainly *explanatory* function, and the tasks serve to clarify and consolidate the points raised. The second section shifts the focus of attention to how the ideas from Section One relate to activities in the classroom. Here the text is concerned with *demonstration*, and the tasks are designed to get readers to evaluate suggestions for teaching in reference both to the ideas from Section One and also to their own teaching experience. In the third section this experience is projected into future work. Here the set of tasks, modelled on those in Section Two, are designed to be carried out by the reader as a combination of teaching techniques and action research in the actual classroom. It is this section that renews the reader's contact with reality: the ideas expounded in Section One and linked to pedagogic practice in Section Two are now to be systematically *tested out* in the process of classroom teaching.

If language teaching is to be a genuinely professional enterprise, it requires continual experimentation and evaluation on the part of practitioners whereby in seeking to be more effective in their pedagogy they provide at the same time—and as a corollary—for their own continuing education. It is our aim in this scheme to promote this dual purpose.

Christopher N. Candlin
Henry Widdowson

Explanation
The principles of evaluation

1 What is evaluation?

1.1 Introduction

It is a common belief that evaluation means the same as testing, and that while students are being tested evaluation is taking place. However, testing is only one component in the evaluation process.

As will be shown, evaluation is an intrinsic part of teaching and learning. It is important for the teacher because it can provide a wealth of information to use for the future direction of classroom practice, for the planning of courses, and for the management of learning tasks and students. The aim of this book is to show practitioners such as language teachers and curriculum developers how useful evaluation is, and how to do it for themselves.

We begin by looking at what is meant by evaluation. If asked the following kind of questions: 'What is evaluation?', 'Why do you want to evaluate something?', or 'What do you want to evaluate?', there is a fairly strong chance that you will think in terms of schools, learners, and examinations. But this is not the only context in which we make judgements about whether something is good or bad, acceptable or unacceptable, or whether something could be improved. Evaluation is not restricted to the context of education; it is a part of our everyday lives.

Evaluation: A natural activity
Consider the way we comment about the weather. The sky may be grey; it may be raining. Alternatively, the sky may be blue with not a cloud in sight. If we then say something like 'What an awful day!' or 'What beautiful weather!' we are engaged in evaluation of an informal kind.

▶ TASK 1

Take a typical day in your life.

1 What sort of things outside your work situation do you make informal evaluative statements about?

2 Now think about your working day. What sort of evaluations do you make about your learners, their work, or your teaching?

3 How are the evaluations in (1) and (2) similar or different?

Evaluation then, is a natural activity; something that is very much part of our daily existence. It is something that can be very formal or informal. It is also something that may not always be made explicit but may actually be undertaken unconsciously. When you listen to a lecture, a radio interview, or a political speech, you are making judgements on many different levels about the speakers. These range from the content of what is being said to thoughts of whether the speaker is kind and generous, honest and reliable, or harsh and uncaring, dishonest and unreliable. Further, as Rowntree (1977:4–5) points out, speakers are constantly responding to what they take to be the emerging attitudes and understandings of other people, and deciding what to say in consequence. In other words, we are constantly making evaluations of one kind or another and modifying our behaviour accordingly.

Making evaluative judgements is therefore a feature of social life, but evaluation is not always something that we do in a *principled* and *systematic* way. The criteria we use in making judgements may sometimes be vague and ill-defined.

1.2 Evaluation in education

When we evaluate different aspects of the teaching and learning process, it becomes important to make explicit the criteria used in our judgements, and to be principled in our evaluations. Ill-prepared and ad-hoc evaluations are likely to be unreliable, unfair, and uninformative. They are not a suitable source on which to base educational decisions. Making decisions about a teacher at work in the classroom will involve a different set of evaluation criteria from those needed to evaluate a set of learning tasks. An evaluation of teacher performance will also be structured differently from an analysis of learner performance. In many ways this is not so different from the judgements we make on other matters, which also involve different criteria at different times for different purposes.

Evaluation and decision making

When we talk about the weather, sport, or fashion, we are not engaged in evaluation for purposes of making decisions that may have some major effect on an individual's life. However, in the educational context the results of a test may determine whether a learner moves into a higher class, or stays down and repeats a year, or whether a teacher will or will not be promoted. The decisions we make regarding a textbook may affect whether or not there is to be widespread use of that text in a school. Thus, the implications of evaluation in an educational setting are potentially far more powerful than those we make in informal social settings. As a result, it becomes crucial that careful thought is given to make explicit what it is we are evaluating, and the criteria by which we judge whether something is 'very good', 'adequate', or 'inadequate' must be clearly identified. Evaluation in an educational context should be systematic and undertaken according to certain guiding principles using carefully defined criteria.

Evaluation in the educational process

It is important to be sure when we mention the need to evaluate our language teaching methods, our materials, our effectiveness as teachers and so on, that we actually know what it is we are evaluating. How materials are presented to learners, the types of learning tasks used, and the way that we design our courses, all form different aspects of our work as teachers. They are all part of the curriculum, of the full *range* of activities which take place both prior to and during the implementation of a learning programme. And they must be evaluated.

Evaluation has a different overall focus and several different purposes from student assessment. While evaluation may be seen as a 'means' analysis (it is intended to serve the learning process), student assessment has a much more limited perspective with a focus on the 'ends' of learning in terms of what the learner has achieved at particular points.

Example: structural and communicative courses

The evaluation of a particular course is one type of evaluation that may be undertaken. Perhaps you have changed from a 'structural' approach to a more 'communicative' one and you want to find out whether learners do better in the new communicative programme. There are a number of different ways in which you could evaluate the relative merits of the new programme. A fairly standard practice has been to compare two groups of learners, that is, one group who have been exposed to the new approach with a second group who continue to be taught using the old, in this case 'structural', approach. At the end of a term a test is administered to both groups of learners and the results are compared.

Imagine that you get the following results:

Communicative course	*Structural course*
Learners pass the test	Learners fail the test
(Average score=59%)	(Average score=45%)

These results show that the learners on the 'communicative' programme did well and passed the test, whereas those who followed the 'structural' programme got below fifty per cent and failed the test. In other words, those learners who took the new programme did better than those who did not.

One interpretation of these results would be that the 'communicative' teaching and learning programme was successful, and that because the course was good, and because both teachers and students did what was required of them by the programme, this led to the 'result' of students passing the test. But is this the only interpretation?

▶   TASK 2

1 Do you think that the evaluation results provide any evidence that the communicative programme works?

2 What other factors do you think could account for these results?

In fact, a range of different conditions may be contributed to the above result. The assessment of learners on tests does not help us very much in identifying with precision what it is that makes learning successful or, conversely, what it is that contributes to unsuccessful learning. More specifically, from a course evaluation we would expect not only to understand better what is good and bad about the programme, but also to gain feedback in terms of an explanation as to which factors contribute to the 'good' and to the 'not so good' aspects of the programme.

It can be shown, for example, that other factors such as the specific teaching methodology, the individual qualities of the teacher, or the learners' exposure to English outside the classroom environment, may have resulted in the improved learner performance on the 'communicative' programme. We cannot be sure what brought about the desired improvement if the only evaluation data we have is limited to a set of test results showing that one group of students outperformed the other group on a single occasion. Such information does not tell us *why* we obtained that particular result or if that result would be repeated. Hence, we need to examine alternative ways of evaluating courses.

Evaluation of process and product
One of the disadvantages of assessments at the end of a term or a teaching year is that you are unable to recapture what has taken place during a programme of instruction. Without information gathered during the process of teaching, you are unable to say *why* learners have done better. The fact that a course of instruction is labelled 'communicative' does not mean that the teaching that actually takes place is communicative. It could be the case that teachers are provided with a new 'communicative' teachers' book, but do not actually change their teaching methodology accordingly. Thus, unless a teacher is interviewed and classroom observation is included in the evaluation procedures, one cannot be sure that any observed learner improvement is a result of changed classroom practice.

In other words, if we are to make valid statements about improvements caused by a particular type of course or by a new textbook, then we need to examine what it is that actually happens during the new course or during the use of the new textbook. When comparing, for example, different methods or learning materials, we should be able to document how new practice differs from previous practice (see **2.4** and **3.3**).

This raises the issue of the 'process' on the one hand and the 'product' of teaching and learning on the other. Results on tests can be interpreted in terms of learner 'products'. They provide an indication of *what* learners can do at any given time. But also of interest to those involved in an evaluation is *how* learners acquire the language proficiency demonstrated by their performance on a test. It follows, therefore, that the process of learning is more relevant when evaluating the extent to which a particular course of instruction is effective and efficient. In other words, as evaluators we should be attempting to identify the processes which lead to successful, or unsuccessful, learning. This will involve us in systematic and principled observations of classroom behaviour. Knowing merely that a learner has passed or failed a test does not help us to understand what worked well, or what did not work well. It is an analysis of what goes on in the classroom that may provide insights into what makes learning successful.

▶ ## TASK 3

From what you have read so far, summarize what you understand to be the main limitations of using test results as a means of evaluating the strengths and weaknesses of two textbooks, one structural and the other more communicative in orientation.

Summary
Two main points emerge from an analysis of the examples given here. The first is that we cannot infer a direct causal relationship between a teaching programme and test results. Secondly, if we are to compare teaching programmes, then we need to have definite criteria for establishing the superiority of one programme over another. We should not assert that one course is better than another unless we have data to show us the ways in which it is superior. Evaluation, in practice, uses a range of different criteria, taking into consideration all sorts of factors derived from our varied teaching and learning situations. It thus becomes necessary to identify more precisely those aspects of the curriculum of potential interest to the evaluator, and the ways in which evaluation may be done.

Before we do this, however, two other issues immediately arise. In the first place, we need to question in more detail why we need evaluation and what it is for. Secondly, we need to consider how to organize and manage evaluation. These issues require us to examine two other concepts that are extricably bound up with evaluation, namely, the notions of (1) innovation or change, and (2) the management of change. These are examined next.

1.3 Evaluation and innovation

Confirming the validity of classroom practice
Evaluation may be planned for two main reasons. One motivation is its use as a means of *explaining* and *confirming* existing procedures. In this

case, evaluation is used to obtain feedback about classroom practice. The aim is to explore the reasons why something is working well in the classroom and why it is appropriate for a given target audience. Evaluation, according to this first meaning, is used to confirm the validity of features of the classroom context. Here, the evaluator seeks to justify existing practice through an explanation of what happens during the teaching and learning event.

Innovation or change?
A second motivation for evaluation is to gain information to bring about *innovation* or *change* (the term innovation implying a planned change). Evaluation and innovation are therefore closely related concepts, with evaluation forming a basis for a subsequent change or modification within the curriculum. Innovation may relate to the introduction of something large in scale, such as a new textbook. Alternatively, it may refer to something much smaller in scale such as a new procedure for the development of listening skills with learners who are beginning English. Whatever the nature of the innovation, it should result from an evaluation of some kind.

Of course changes take place for which there has been no planned evaluation. In fact, a large number of changes in our teaching contexts occur in an unsystematic fashion. But innovation should be planned and managed. The process of evaluation can usefully inform the nature and implementation of an innovation.

To take one example, in a certain country the following happened. Inspectors and teachers were unhappy with the existing textbooks. The Ministry of Education decided to replace them with more appropriate books for secondary schools. Much of the initial work focused on a principled evaluation of the existing textbooks in order to find out their strengths and weaknesses. To this end, teachers' opinions were solicited through regional seminars and inspectors also played an important role through their classroom observations. The views of learners were also sought through class interviews. Using these procedures, the good points of the existing books were highlighted, such as the clear pictures, the appropriateness of level and topics of the reading texts, and the types of pronunciation activities. The inadequacies of the books were also detailed, such as the way in which the vocabulary was presented in the form of wordlists, the predominance of teacher-controlled learning exercises with no opportunity for learners to engage in communicative activities, and the overall poor layout of the books. It also became clear that a set of teachers' books was needed since the existing provision was limited to a syllabus listing the grammatical items to be covered each year which provided no other guidance to the teacher.

▶ TASK 4

    1 Consider your own teaching and learning context. Make a list of any innovations you can think of that have taken place in the past or that are taking place now.

    2 For the innovations you list, state whether an evalution was carried out as a basis for the innovations themselves.

The example above used evaluation in order to introduce something new into the English curriculum. Evaluation may also be useful to determine whether or not present classroom practices are working. Take the example of some teachers who attended an in-service course where different ways of developing writing skills were introduced. On returning to their schools, they decided to try out a few of the ideas presented, in particular those which focused on preparing learners for writing and the organization of written work. One way of evaluating whether these new techniques actually worked in class was through observation. This observation focused on questions such as the following:

1 Did most of the learners understand the instructions?

2 Did most of the learners take part in the group activities which analysed the topic?

3 Did the learners use more English through this technique than they usually do?

4 Was the learners' written work better organized than usual?

5 Did the learners have less difficulty in finding something to write about than usual?

6 Did the learners seem to enjoy the preparation for the writing task?

Positive answers to questions like these would confirm that the new approach was working. Information provided by an evaluation of this kind would indicate to the teachers the value of trying out new approaches, and clarify what actually works and what does not work in their classrooms.

▶ TASK 5

Consider your own teaching and learning context. Indicate two or three areas you would like to evaluate as a means of confirming that present practice is appropriate for your learners.

The two main reasons for undertaking an evaluation are illustrated as follows:

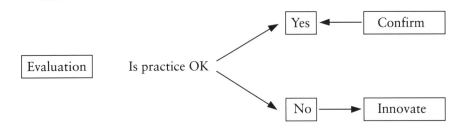

Figure 1 *Reasons for evaluation*

Teachers therefore need to consider two different things. By monitoring aspects of their classroom practice in order to evaluate the validity of what they are doing, they are able to identify reasons why some things work well and others do not. On the one hand, the teachers are engaged in a process which confirms that the existing practice is appropriate. On the other, they will be able to use the evaluation data as a basis for suggesting change. In these respects evaluation is always to some degree innovative, and implies a dynamic process. In this book, then, we are concerned with principled evaluation procedures with a view either to confirming the appropriacy of what we do in classrooms or to introducing innovations in our teaching and learning contexts.

Evaluation criteria
As we have seen earlier, it is important to be able to identify those factors that contribute to classroom successes. We must be specific about the criteria used to judge whether something works. If we are dissatisfied with an aspect of our work, for example the textbook, or the nature of learner participation in class, or the kind of classroom activities used to promote oral skills, or even the syllabus itself, we should be able to clarify precisely what it is that leads to our dissatisfaction.

▶ TASK 6

Are you completely satisfied with the textbook you use for your teaching?

1 Make a list of the strengths of this particular book and then a list of its weaknesses.

2 What criteria did you use to identify the strengths and the weaknesses of your textbook?

Without information obtained from a systematic evaluation of, say, a textbook, it is hard to plan for something that is actually better, that is designed to bring about the desired improvements.

Innovations, however, sometimes prove unpopular and do not work. It is therefore important to understand some of the reasons for this. It is also the case that an innovation may work for some people but not for others. At this point it is useful to explore the notion of innovation in a little more detail.

Introducing an innovation
The issue of how an innovation is introduced and implemented is crucial. Sometimes there is insufficient dialogue with the users of the innovation before it is introduced. For example, a new set of tests may be imposed on classroom teachers without adequate explanation as to how they are to be used and marked, and the following may result. The new system is not understood by some teachers and they decide not to have anything to do with it. Some teachers may try to use the new testing procedures but because they have an inadequate grasp of them, they make mistakes and subsequently decide to return to their old methods. Other teachers see the new system as a move to undermine their authority and so dismiss it out of hand. Thus, there may be resistance to something new not only because it has not been fully explained but also because it is viewed as something external which does not belong to the teachers themselves. As a consequence, they may be reluctant to make adjustments to their current classroom practices and reject the innovation.

Let us consider ways in which the introduction of an innovation may be approached.

The research, development, and diffusion model
The tests and the new textbook examples above reflect an approach to the management of innovation that is often referred to as the research, development, and diffusion model (henceforth RD and D). It is an approach that has been, and still is, widely used. Features associated with this model are that it is initiated by an agent external to the teaching situation, for example by a department of the Ministry of Education, largely without consultation with teachers; that it is felt that the innovation is a 'good thing' and that the individuals with the relevant expertise are those in the Ministry. Thus teachers, who will be expected to implement the innovation, are excluded from the planning process. Frequently outside 'experts' may be called in to assist with the innovation. Textbook writing has often been managed in this way.

▶ TASK 7

Think of your own educational situation.

1 Can you think of any innovations that have taken place following the RD and D model?

2 Briefly describe the innovation and explain why you think the RD and D model was used.

In addition to external initiation, planning, and management, the RD and D model implies a directive style, poor access to information, high demands in terms of financial resources, and minimal communication between the planners and the teachers who will be expected to implement the innovation, whether it be a new syllabus, textbook, methodology, or testing procedure.

There are, however, alternatives to the RD and D model. Indeed, this approach may itself be modified to incorporate aspects of other approaches to the management of innovation.

The social interaction model
The social interaction model of innovation is one in which there is an emphasis on user involvement, with the teacher taking an active part in the innovation process. Accordingly, the planning and management of the innovation may be carried out by a number of different people or groups. This may, for example, include teachers, the relevant departments in a Ministry of Education, the Examinations Council, the Teacher Training College, the relevant university departments or representatives from an English Panel, and so on. This approach is collective and collaborative and recognizes that a range of contributions are relevant to the introduction of something new in the English language curriculum.

▶ TASK 8

Examine the following characteristics of approaches to innovation:

centralized	expensive	easy access to information
directive	collaborative	poor access to information
individual enquiries	consultative	flexible
top down approach	feedback	teacher participation
outside experts	prescriptive	variety of contributors
decentralised	team work	responsive to user needs

Which of the characteristics above do you most identify with (1) the RD and D model, and (2) the social interaction model of innovation?

It is now less likely that you will come across a pure example of one of the models. A combination of characteristics associated with each of the approaches to the management of innovation is much more likely.

▶ TASK 9

Consider innovations that have taken place in your own educational context.

1 Have any been introduced using the social interaction approach or aspects of this approach?

2 Briefly describe the innovation and explain why you think this approach was used.

Compare your answers with those to Task 7. Which is the predominant model for innovation used? Can you suggest reasons why this might be so?

A third model is that of 'action research', which is a teacher-driven approach to classroom innovation. By definition it is highly relevant to the needs of the classroom as it involves evaluation working upwards from the classroom level. This is discussed in **3.4**.

Evaluation need not have all the trappings of an expensive project. Through the involvement of teachers, learners, and inspectors, it can be operated locally on a small scale. It is not necessary to construct an expensive, high status, large-scale evaluation, and the value of small local initiatives is now being increasingly recognized.

Innovation is a phenomenon that has always been part of good teaching, but for it to be carried out effectively there is a need for teachers to raise their consciousness of classroom practices and to formalize this in some manner. Through evaluation this may be achieved.

► # TASK 10

To what extent have the innovations you described in Tasks 7 and 9 been successful? What reasons do you attribute to the successes and the failures?

Maximum involvement of relevant groups is now seen as a key factor in the development, acceptance, and success of an innovation. We shall return in more detail to the ways in which teachers and other professionals can become involved in initiating innovation in the classroom in **3.4**.

Summary
Some of the successes and failures of the innovation process are closely related to the ways in which innovation has been managed. There are different ways in which, for example, a new textbook can be introduced into schools. Some of these work, others do not. The acceptance of a new approach to in-service training in a country is usually largely attributable to the ways in which this innovation has been managed. Successful innovation requires good management, securing maximum cooperation and involvement among all the groups concerned.

Thus, approaches to introducing and planning for innovation have close links with concepts of management and leadership, to the extent that an evaluation has to be planned and executed by a number of different people. This is considered in more detail in the next section.

1.4 Evaluation and management

Evaluation contributes to the good management of teaching and learning. It too must be well managed. Good management practice integrates both continuous and final evaluation into any educational and teaching plan.

The teacher as manager

What does 'the teacher as manager' mean? For some people it means directing learners towards getting a task done effectively or guiding them towards personal learning strategies. But the expression can mean other things. For example, in schools, and more specifically in classrooms, good management includes dealing with financial, material, and physical, as well as human resources. What, then, does it take for a teacher to be a good manager? Can evaluation illuminate the practice of good teaching management? Everard (1986:127) outlines some characteristics of a good manager, which have been adapted to the language teaching context:

Managerial qualities	Language teaching context (examples)
To know what s/he wants to happen and cause it to happen	Developing aims and objectives of a lesson or sequence
To exercise responsibility over resources and turn them to purposeful account	Making effective use of resources
To promote effectiveness in work and search for continual improvement	Motivating learners towards better learning strategies
To be accountable for the performance of the unit s/he is managing	Being accountable to parents, heads, learners
To set a climate or tone conducive to enabling people to give of their best	Establishing rapport with learners and maintaining good classroom organization

Table 1 *Managerial qualities for language teaching (after Everard 1986:127)*

The practice of management is closer to the work of teachers and others responsible for education than we realize. Management skills are necessary when teachers make decisions on classroom organization and resource allocation, discipline, organizing pair work, group discussion, and so on.

▶ TASK 11

What other practical examples can you think of that require the teacher to exercise management skills?

Good management of teaching and learning includes evaluation. You cannot manage properly if you do not monitor. For example, if you set up a group discussion you need to evaluate its effectiveness while it is happening and you may decide to intervene to keep the discussion on course. Or you may decide to evaluate the activity and performance later in the context of the whole lesson with a view to improving your own planning. Running a class without evaluating its effectiveness is bad management practice.

Management in language teaching: leadership

In education the management of human resources is a key issue and leadership plays a vital role. Good leadership includes an evaluation component: teaching tasks themselves must be evaluated and teachers, too, must evaluate themselves performing these tasks. We can look again at Everard's list (see Table 1) and notice two managerial characteristics which indicate a real need for leadership qualities and skills: (1) promoting effectiveness and continual improvement, and (2) creating a climate which enables people to give of their best. If we take everyday classroom examples—arranging the classroom, giving instructions, or choosing the content of the lesson—teachers are already exercising essential leadership skills. Can this be developed in other areas? Evaluation by teachers themselves can point in the right direction.

▶ ## TASK 12

From your personal teaching experience:

1 What do you think are the most important features in managing people? Write down a short list.

2 What affective and other factors do you take into account when managing the classroom, for example competitiveness, motivation, personal interests, and problems?

Our classroom experience as educators can contribute much to a better understanding of good leadership. We are already exercising leadership skills according to our understanding of what it means to be a teacher in a particular teaching context. It is relevant here to ask, 'Are some people born to be leaders or it is a question of skill and craft?'

Basic characteristics of leaders

Some basic characteristics of classroom leadership emerge from the findings of leadership research (Bryman 1986). Leadership skills are founded on personal qualities. Thus, to some extent teachers are born not made. However, personal qualities can be developed and strengthened.

Personal qualities
1 personal self-awareness
2 professional integrity
3 person-oriented (welfare)
4 organized planning
5 openness and naturalness with a sense of humour
6 personal presence and authority

Table 2 *Personal qualities (Germaine 1989)*

Personal qualities include being aware of one's own strengths, for example being patient and tolerant, and weaknesses, for example not being organized or punctual. Strengths and weaknesses show up in the classroom in the way in which we respond to slow learners, plan lessons, and so on.

Leadership skills, on the other hand, show up in the way that teachers handle the teaching group based on their experience, how they can handle crisis in the classroom, and how they help learners to interact with each other. The following table relates general leadership styles to the language classroom.

Styles of leadership	Language teaching context
	Examples
1 Autocratic	Teacher-centred; teacher imposes decisions on class
2 Paternalistic	Teacher 'sells' decisions to class
3 Consultative	Decisions subject to questioning and change
4 Participative	Teacher presents problem, gets suggestions, and decides
5 Democratic	Class functions within limits defined by teacher
6 Person-oriented	Learner-centred; teacher takes account of individual learners
7 Task-oriented	Syllabus must be completed
8 Contingency	Teacher adapts to the changing needs of individual learners, the class, and to the demands of the syllabus

Table 3 *Styles of leadership in the language teaching context*

As suggested in Table 3, autocratic leadership reflects a teacher-centred approach whereas a learner-centred approach is more participative and democratic in outlook.

Evaluation can be used to monitor the strengths and weaknesses in teachers' leadership skills, and to provide an indication of whether these skills are working appropriately and whether the styles of leadership are responding to changing circumstances. Teachers are often expected to make management decisions concerning their classes, for example whether to carry on with a new activity they have planned or spend more time in remedial work. Evaluation helps us to decide where priorities lie: with the task or people? A dilemma exists: (task) should we concentrate on getting the work done, for example pursuing the syllabus, or (people) should we gear classes to the learners' level and pace, for example each learner's own syllabus. Further, external pressures of context may exist in the form of a national syllabus, formal examinations, parents' expectations, and so on.

▶ TASK 13

　1　How would you describe yourself in terms of leadership styles? Refer to Table 3 above.

　2　Evaluate what style best suits your own situation. Can you explain why?

Leadership styles, then, have implications for language teaching management. For example, in the learner-centred approach those in charge take learners' needs into account and teachers can involve learners in decision making. This approach and shared involvement can result in better courses and improved commitment to work. And evaluation can keep these objectives in true perspective.

A balanced approach to leadership in language teaching
In language teaching, we do not work in isolation but in institutional contexts, for example, schools, colleges, and departments. Contingency leadership (see item 8, Table 3) offers a balanced model for language teaching, as shown in the following summary.

1　In the classroom teachers prioritize between the task, group, and individual according to the demands of the situation. This flexibility means, of course, that at any moment they can be task-oriented, group-oriented or individual-oriented.

2　Task functions directed towards task needs contain activities like setting objectives, allocating responsibilities, and deciding appropriate standards.

3　Group maintenance functions deal with team building and motivation, communication, etc.

4　Individual maintenance is geared towards coaching, counselling, self-development, etc.
　(Cole 1983)

▶ **TASK 14**

Think of a recent teaching experience. Evaluate how you dealt with the class according to the contingency principles above.

1 What was the task and how did you maintain it?

2 How did you get individuals to work together and to create a group spirit?

3 Did you have to deal with individual problems? What were they and how did you handle them?

Good leadership in language teaching management is crucial and can vary according to the situation. The contingency approach is a flexible, balanced approach which responds creatively to changing needs, especially of the learner. It demands frequent evaluation of changing learner needs and the teacher's response to these.

▶ **TASK 15**

1 Imagine you are in a seminar group with colleagues discussing learner-centredness and teacher-centredness. How would you describe your own style of leadership in the classroom? Write down an outline description.

2 When you initiate a classroom innovation how do you involve learners?

Good management of human resources has its effect on other aspects of language teaching management, to which we now turn our attention.

Management in language teaching: aims, materials, and accountability
In the first item in Everard's list (see Table 1, page 14), we see that teachers as managers should be clear about the aims of their classes. In lesson planning teachers set the aims of the lesson in the light of the sequence of lessons, the level of the learners, and the demands of the syllabus. They need to plan materials to use and timing for each part of the lesson, and anticipate the kinds of interaction that may occur during the lesson.

Evaluation has its part to play in all these aspects. In the course of the lesson teachers monitor the effectiveness of the materials (Are the instructions clear?), and timing (Should I spend more time on a grammar point?), and the motivation of the learners (Are the learners interested?). Teachers also evaluate their own performance (Were my aims achieved? Did all the parts of the lesson fit together logically?).

The effective use of resources may include utilizing all available materials, such as books, board, magazines, and technical equipment. It may also include searching out new resources. Evaluation can help the teacher examine whether any current resources are being underused, for example unused audio tapes, and where new aids can be found, for example attending a language materials workshop. To illustrate the value of evaluation, an assessment of a small picture library can involve asking:

1 How often have I used pictures in my lesson?
2 Have I used them effectively as an aid to learning?
3 Are they up to date (e.g. photos of famous people)?

Summary
Evaluation is essential to good management. Evaluation gives impetus to leadership and promotes a professional approach to managing teaching and learning resources. Evaluation can be informal, with teachers evaluating the ways they manage their own classrooms, or it can be planned more extensively and involve school or project management. The context in which we work as teachers will influence the ways in which we carry out evaluations. We shall consider this next.

1.5 Evaluation and context

Definition
The relationship between evaluation and the context in which evaluations are undertaken is of fundamental importance. Context consists of a range of aspects beginning with the socio-cultural environment and political considerations, which includes the politics of the education system, moving through to all those involved in the process of education: directors of education, inspectors, learners, teachers, and so on. This can be illustrated as follows:

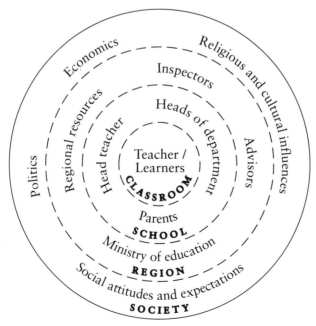

Figure 2 *A context for evaluation*

▶ TASK 16

1 Using Figure 2 as a guide, what important factors influence your own teaching and learning context?

2 Evaluate their relative importance in that process and any problems that arise.

A teacher does not live and work in an isolated environment. The classroom is itself a context influenced by the individuals in it. Group interaction affects the climate of the classroom. A school has its own organizational culture. The school is situated within a regional setting which in turn is part of a larger social and political environment with its own outlook on education. Views on education range from seeing it as training manpower, transmission of culture, social control, or individual development. All these things influence both directly and indirectly how language is taught, learned, and evaluated in the classroom.

The role of evaluation
Evaluation makes teachers aware of the parameters in which they are working. Raising awareness in this way helps them to analyse the context for possible openings for innovation or for constraints. It illuminates the effects that society has on the personal behaviour of the teacher and learners, and on classroom interaction. For example, if a society tends to be authoritarian, it is likely to be reflected in the classroom environment. It affects the roles of teachers and learners (autocratic, teacher-centred approaches as distinct from participative, learner-centred approaches). Analysing contexts helps teachers to evaluate possible approaches for their classrooms.

Interplay between evaluation and context
The context affects evaluation
As we have seen earlier, evaluation can identify areas for curriculum improvement, including modifications to classroom methodology or learning materials. Evaluation can raise awareness of the need for change and also where change can take place. However, it is possible to manage effective innovation in a variety of ways and there is no one right way of doing this. It varies from context to context, dependent on one, some, or all of the influences identified in Figure 2.

The context in which we teach will modify any innovation: how it is introduced, implemented, and evaluated. Evaluation, therefore, is directly affected by context. Its scope can be broad or narrow depending on the resources of the context or the outlook of the people concerned. In some situations, for example in decentralized educational systems, the onus is on the individual school, or even the individual teacher, to make curriculum adjustments. This is quite acceptable in that context. On the other hand, where there is considerable government or ministry control of the educational system, a move by an individual teacher to introduce innovation in the classroom might be considered revolutionary, and such a move might be counterproductive. The findings of evaluations have to be interpreted in the light of the entire socio-cultural and political context in which the teaching and learning take place.

▶ TASK 17

Think of some change you would like in your classroom.

1 What factors in your context would make change difficult to implement?

2 What factors would support and sustain this change?

Obvious constraints such as class size or layout make innovation difficult. How you evaluate your communicative method is influenced by the environment of the class which is a feature of your context. Supportive factors might include close working relations between inspectors and teachers or support groups among the teachers themselves, or a well stocked learning resources centre.

Evaluation affects the context
Evaluation can break the cycle of old influences and initiate new ones. In some circumstances there may be an uneasy relationship between education and society as represented by culture, religion, and politics. The relationship itself is undoubtedly complex but the uneasiness may be highlighted simply. Society may see education's role as one of preserving its values while cautiously advancing within defined limits. However, educationists may take a less conservative approach and view their role as one of broadening the horizons and experiences of learners, making use of a rich variety of sources.

▶ TASK 18

1 Write a brief outline of any evaluation in which you participated and which resulted in a change in your classroom practice.

2 Did this change influence the context? How?

Often more authoritarian systems see evaluation as a means of control. If an evaluation is undertaken in order to make people more accountable for their work, an underlying need to maintain power may be hidden. The situation becomes suspicious when, having initiated an evaluation (dressed up as appraisal), those representing the authoritarian system are unwilling to accept the consequences, especially when the outcomes imply serious change throughout. For example, take the case of a college senior management which set up an evaluation of the quality of teaching. Implied in the evaluation is that the focus of attention is on the teaching staff. One hidden purpose may be to find reasons to increase class contact hours. However, after an honest evaluation, one of the outcomes is that the quality of teaching is suffering because the staff are not provided with enough resources and have insufficient in-service training. This implies change which costs money. It also implies that management is not managing the resources of the college properly and that their work needs to be appraised for efficiency. Evaluation may be a double-edged sword.

Evaluation questions preconceived assumptions, sometimes to confirm them but also to dismantle them. This is one reason why evaluation is often disliked or seen as suspect, and why there are sometimes difficulties for the evaluators themselves. Most societies and institutions demonstrate dynamic conservatism (Everard and Morris 1990); they actively resist change. Yet evaluation can be the instrument of necessary innovation, in turn creating 'new contexts'.

1.6 Summary

We have seen in this first section that evaluation means much more than administering tests to learners and analysing the results. Evaluation is a useful tool for the practitioner, whether teacher, materials writer, or inspector. As a concept, it is not something that is new to us; in our everyday lives we are continuously making judgements. Evaluation is also a regular part of a teacher's professional work. But are we always aware that we are making evaluative judgements?

Evaluation of our educational practices is varied and covers a wide range of issues. Focusing merely on learner performance does not provide an explanation as to why something works or why something does not. We should also evaluate the process of teaching in order to develop insights into ways in which aspects of teaching can be improved. Using evaluation activities we can also confirm the validity of what we do in the classroom and develop ways in which we can seek to understand better the processes, for example, types of materials, particular methods, or learner involvement, which lead to successful teaching and learning.

Successful evaluation should be systematic and principled. In order to achieve this we need to take into account the concept of management as reflected through our leadership skills. As teachers we need to be aware of our role as managers and evaluate our management styles. We need to know why we wish to evaluate, what evaluation is for, and how to organize it. These issues are explored further in the sections that follow.

2 Purposes for evaluation

2.1 Introduction

A number of different purposes for evaluation can be identified. They can be divided into two broad categories:

1 general purposes
2 specific, topic-related purposes.

The main general purposes are examined first.

2.2 General evaluation purposes

Evaluation may be undertaken for three principal reasons:

1 accountability
2 curriculum development and betterment
3 self-development: teachers and other language teaching professionals.

▶ TASK 19

Read the following statements. Which of the three purposes for evaluation given above can you identify?

1 The standards of language teaching in schools will be evaluated by comparing results from the end of year examinations.

2 Our aim is to encourage teachers to look at, describe, and understand what happens in their classrooms. In teaching vocabulary, for example, do they: use visual aids wherever possible? present the vocabulary within a context? translate meanings into the learners' mother tongue? introduce a maximum of twelve new words in any one lesson? Do they allow learners to use their mother tongue?

3 Before we make suggestions about increasing the use of visual aids in the classroom, we need to gather information about what types teachers use at the moment and at what point in the lesson they are being used.

4 The textbook I use is a structural one. The writing exercises mainly involve the manipulation of structure. I want to try out

some different ways of giving learners the opportunity for more free writing practice. I will then need to analyse how effective the new tasks are.

5 Fifteen months ago we introduced a new reading scheme into the school. Next week we are having a consultant to evaluate whether it has worked or not.

Evaluation for purposes of accountability
Evaluation for purposes of accountability is mainly concerned with determining whether there has been value for money, in other words whether something has been both effective and efficient. The main aim is to report on a product and give an evaluative judgement, whether something is intrinsically a 'good thing' or not. Generally the information derived from evaluation for purposes of accountability is not used in any major way to improve the functioning of the curriculum or classroom practice. Rather it informs decisions as to whether something is to continue or be discontinued. If, for example, sponsors or heads of institutions are not satisfied with the implementation of a particular project, then cuts may be made. Thus, if a particular reading scheme is introduced, evaluated a year later, and then judged to be ineffective, it is highly likely that a school will discontinue supporting this venture.

▶ TASK 20

1 Describe any accountability evaluations conducted within your own teaching and learning context. Were you or any of your colleagues consulted? Did you contribute to the evaluation in any way?

2 Can you think of a situation where evaluation for accountability is necessary?

Evaluations of this type are largely, although not exclusively, the domain of policy makers or providers of resources. As the above quotation makes explicit, there is a close link between power and evaluation for accountability. There are other points to notice. Usually, such evaluations are carried out after an innovation has been running for some time, or at the end of a project. This type of evaluation, known as *summative evaluation*, has also tended to involve testing and measurement, and analyses of the statistical significance of results obtained. It has focused on the overall outcomes, i.e. end product of an innovation, and has consistently failed to take into account teachers' evaluative comments. Summative evaluations are limited by their focus on outcomes at the end of an educational innovation.

Evaluation for purposes of curriculum development

Teachers have a key role to play in the curriculum renewal and development process. The ideas of Stenhouse (1975) were pivotal in placing classroom practice at the forefront of curriculum enquiries.

▶ # TASK 21

Read the following quotation from Stenhouse (1975:105) about the evaluation of the Schools Council Science 5–13 project and then answer the questions below.

'From the first set of trials it was learned that information coming from children's test results was tentative and not readily usable for guiding rewriting without being supplemented by other data. The results played a useful part in confirming that the general approach of the materials was effective in promoting achievement of its stated objectives, and the development of tests also had side-benefits for the production of Units. But for indicating changes which would make the Units more effective they were of much less use than information from other sources . . .

Whilst it could not be said that the test information was without value for this Project, it can be said that where resources are limited and it is necessary to concentrate upon gathering information to give the greatest return on money, time and human energy, then the choice would be for teachers' reports and direct observations in the classroom and not for tests of short-term changes in children's behaviour.'
(Harlen 1973:91–92 cited in Stenhouse 1975)

1 How useful were the test results in this evaluation? What were their shortcomings?

2 Why do you think teachers' reports are considered to be so valuable?

Evaluation for curriculum development purposes will involve information from teachers and other relevant ELT professionals. As we saw in **1.3**, it is important in the management of evaluation to include all relevant parties. From this it follows that teachers have major contributions to make in the evaluation of classrooms. It is the teacher, rather than the 'tester' or the evaluation 'expert', who has most information about specific classroom contexts. This information may be reported at various times and in various forms, for example as responses to questionnaires, interviews, records, or diary keeping (see **3.3**). It may be largely descriptive and qualitative, and need not entail tests, measurements, and inferences about curriculum quality from statistical data. In contrast to summative evaluation for purposes of accountability, evaluations intended to improve the curriculum will gather information from different people over a period of time. This is known as *formative evaluation*. Such evaluations are ongoing and monitor developments by identifying the strengths and weaknesses of all aspects of teaching and learning. As opposed to merely passing an evaluative judgement on the end product of a teaching programme (summative evaluation), formative evaluation is designed to provide information that may be used as the basis for future planning and action. It is formative since it aims to strengthen and improve the curriculum.

Evaluation for purposes of teacher self-development

A third and major role that evaluation has to play is in formalizing and extending a teacher's knowledge about teaching and learning in classrooms. This is sometimes referred to as *illuminative evaluation* (Parlett and Hamilton 1987) because it involves raising the consciousness of teachers and other ELT practitioners as to what actually happens (as opposed to what is supposed to happen) in the language teaching classroom. This type of evaluation is also developmental and formative.

▶ **TASK 22**

Think about what you do in a reading lesson. Use the following questions to guide you.

Using a reading text:

1 What is done with the text itself?
   learners read silently?
   learners read aloud?
   teacher reads aloud?
   other:

2 How are the questions in the reading text used?
   learners talk about the topic of the text?
   ignore the questions at first?
   learners read the questions before reading the text?
   learners read the text first then the questions?
   the teacher reads the questions out loud?
   learners answer individually by putting hand up?
   learners work in groups and collect answers?

Evaluation of this kind is definitely not concerned with measurement. Through awareness-raising activities, teachers are involved in describing and better understanding their own contexts with a view to improving the teaching and learning process. Such evaluations are both illuminative and formative in purpose. They focus more on the process, and less on the product, of teaching and learning and have a major role to play in teacher self-development.

Summary

In this section we have examined the general purposes for evaluation (accountability, curriculum development, and teacher self-development). Accountability is usually linked with summative evaluation while curriculum development and teacher self-development are better informed by evaluation as a formative process.

The next section examines specific topic-related aspects of the language teaching curriculum which can usefully be evaluated.

2.3 Specific topic-related purposes for evaluation

A general indication of why we evaluate has been offered in the preceding pages. Here, we examine ways in which evaluation is important to classroom teachers and how their awareness can be raised by evaluation activities. We are concerned with formative and illuminative evaluation, associated with curriculum development and teacher self-development.

What is meant by the *environment* of the classroom since it is this that provides the focus for our evaluations? The environment is made up of many things including the social organization of the classroom, the textbooks, the mode(s) of teacher presentation, and the resources available to the teacher. Thus, when we ask the question 'Do our teaching and learning programmes work?' (i.e. are they effective?), we need to identify clearly the focus of our question. Are we interested in evaluating the classroom organization, aspects of teacher presentation, or is the focus on the textbook or the way we teach grammar? The evaluator has to be clear as to what is being examined.

In **1.2**, we observed that to evaluate whether a programme works or not depends on more than whether learners can pass a test at the end of the course. In particular we noted that:

1 evaluation is not restricted to the testing of learners' abilities
2 more than just the end product is important when evaluating a learning programme
3 there are different conditions that may explain, or contribute towards an explanation of, why a programme is successful or not
4 other information, related to a range of different aspects of the teaching and learning process, should be included in an evaluation of the curriculum, to complement data typically derived from a test analysis of learner performance.

In other words, the varied processes of teaching are as important as the outcome of learning, and in order to improve learning outcomes, there is a need to examine more closely those conditions that may contribute to successful language learning. What is needed is a detailed examination of the environment created by the teacher and learners to promote effective language learning. Evaluation is the means by which we can gain a better understanding of what is effective, what is less effective, and what appears to be of no use at all. In order to do this, evaluation must focus on both the means and the product of the learning process.

The next section analyses some of the more specific questions that teachers, and other language teaching professionals, may wish to ask of these classroom environments. Teaching and learning materials are examined first.

2.4 Materials

Before analysing the extent to which given teaching and learning materials are suitable, there are preliminary questions to address. The materials selected for classroom use can be defined in a number of ways.

What do materials mean for you?

1 Do you refer exclusively to textbooks, or do you include teachers' guides, teaching manuals, supplementary units, readers, audio and visual materials, etc?
2 Do you make a distinction between materials designed specifically for first and second language teaching, and also between those targeted specifically for use in school and materials that are non-pedagogic but authentic?
3 Do you include materials produced by the teachers and the learners?

The role of materials within your teaching and learning context

1 What role(s) are they expected to play?
2 What goal(s) are they expected to achieve?

How are the materials to be used?

1 Are they to be used as the sole source and resource for teaching?
2 Are they one of several available resources?

▶   TASK 23

With reference to your situation, describe what materials mean for you and how they are used.

An evaluation of materials for your classroom context will reflect your answer to Task 26. As a first step, you need to define 'materials' so that you, and any others involved in the evaluation, can be clear about what is being examined. It need not be a full-blown textbook in every instance. You may be interested in evaluating a small set of tasks, drills, or texts, as illustrated in the next task.

▶ TASK 24

Look at the following questions used to evaluate suitable texts for an EAP (English for Academic Purposes) course:

PURPOSE	Is the purpose clearly defined?
TYPE	Does the type of exercise effectively and economically accomplish the purpose?
CONTENT	Is the ratio of language given/learner task economic?
	Are instructions to learners clear?
INTEREST	Is it interesting?
AUTHENTICITY	Is it a meaningful task?
	Is it challenging?
DIFFICULTY	Does it contain distracting difficulties?

(Moore 1980:49)

1 Are there any other criteria for text selection you would like to add?
2 In what ways would questions like these be useful to you for evaluating materials in your context?

There has been a tendency for overreliance on classroom teaching materials, with unrealistic expectations made of them. However, the effectiveness of teaching and learning is not explained solely in terms of how good or bad the learning materials are. As Allwright (1981) suggests, materials are only *part* of the co-operative management of language learning. It is also crucial not to overemphasize the importance of learning materials.

Evaluation of classroom learning materials

The first way in which materials may be evaluated is in terms of how well they reflect the principles by which they have been written. In the case of class textbooks, the evaluation criteria will be those used when deciding which book is best for your teaching context. When it comes to teacher-made materials a specification, i.e. a list of criteria against which to evaluate the materials, is indicated at the outset—or accumulated during the process of materials writing—and is thus 'known' to the teacher. In both cases, we are referring to the theoretical worth of the materials.

▶ TASK 25

Examine this extract from a 'checklist of evaluation criteria':

> **Presentation and practice of grammar items**
>
> Comment on the presentation of new structures (grammar items).
> How are new structures presented? To what extent is the
> presentation:
>
> related to what has been previously learned?
> meaningful (in context)?
> systematic?
> representative of the underlying grammar rule?
> appropriate to the given context?
> relevant to learners' needs and interests?
>
> Comment on practice activities for new structures. Are they:
>
> adequate in number?
> varied?
> meaningful?
> appropriate to the given context?
> relevant to learners' needs and interests?
> sufficiently controlled?

(after Cunningsworth 1984:76–7)

1 To what extent would the above be useful to you in the analysis
   of the textbook you use?
2 What modifications or additions would you suggest?

When we analyse classroom materials in this way, we are evaluating the
theoretical value, or the 'construct validity', of a set of materials.

What we should note about the example above is that we are examining
the materials as they stand, that is without reference to their actual use in
the classroom. This provides restricted evaluation data since it gives us no
information about how these materials actually work with a class. This
distinction between the theoretical (i.e. construct validity) and empirical
value of materials has been well captured by Breen (1989). Adapting his
diagram we can illustrate the three phases in the evaluation of materials.

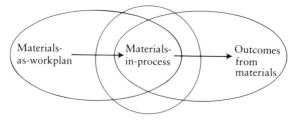

Figure 3 *Three phases of materials evaluation (after Breen 1989)*

We can generalize from the notion of 'tasks' to the notion of teaching and learning materials in the following manner. 'Materials-as-workplan' refers to the theoretical value of materials, taking up the range of points covered in comprehensive checklists such as Cunningsworth's. But, as Breen (1989:189) states:

'Workplans can only provide opportunities for change in knowledge and capability and for successful outcomes in relatively unpredictable and broad measure.'

This brings us to an evaluation of 'Materials-in-process'. This stage generates information about the ways in which learners and teachers actually use and respond to materials, thus providing indicators as to whether the materials are 'successful' or not. The 'Outcomes from materials' represent the relative achievements of learners (see **2.6, 12,** and **13**).

▶   TASK 26

Look at this extract adapted from Cunningworth's checklist of evaluation criteria:

Chapter 7 Motivation and the learner

Does the material have variety and pace?

Is the subject matter of reading texts, listening passages etc. likely to be of genuine interest to the learners, taking into account their age, social background and cultural background, their learning objectives and the composition of the class?

Does the material have an attractive appearance (visuals, layout, typography etc.)?

Do the activities in the material encourage the personal involvement of the learners in the learning process (e.g. by talking about themselves or finding out about each other)?

If material is culture-specific, will this be acceptable to the learners?

Is there a competitive or problem-solving element in the learning activities?

(*Cunningsworth 1984:79*)

1 Do any of these criteria relate to how the materials actually work in the classroom?

2 How would you reword some of these questions so that they would provide information about how the materials were used in a classroom?

Who evaluates the materials is the final point to be considered here. Low (1987) comments on the range of individuals connected with a language learning course and examines both the nature and purpose of the evaluations they are likely to make. For Low, ten different perspectives on materials evaluation could be offered:

> The Learner
> The Parent
> The Teacher
> The Head or College Principal
> The Teacher Trainer
> The Curriculum Committee Member
> The Inspector
> The Educational Researcher
> The Publisher
> The Materials Designer
> *(Low 1987)*

▶ TASK 27

> Choose two from the above list and suggest how and why they might participate.

By examining the role(s) of these participating groups in the materials evaluation process, Low (1987) shows how each group will have different interests and different questions to be answered. For example, a materials writer might carry out a formative evaluation designed to indicate whether the texts are appropriate to the target learners, and then make the necessary changes. A parent, on the other hand, might only be interested in examination results, which implies a summative assessment of learner performance.

On the premise that 'teachers may benefit greatly in the evaluation, design and use of materials by engaging the help and views of learners', Breen and Candlin suggest ways in which learners may participate in the evaluation of materials (see opposite).

Again, as with most inventories of this kind, the questions can be reformulated to make them more relevant to individual contexts.

On the procedures for working with tasks and activities in the classroom

What do you find are the most useful ways to learn a new language?

What are the best kinds of language learning tasks and activities? What are the reasons for your choice?

What can a teacher do which would help you most when you are learning a new language?

What can other learners in the class do which would help you most when you are learning a new language?

What is your favourite kind of language lesson?

What are the reasons for your choice?

What are the good things and the bad things about learning a language in a classroom?

What can materials best provide you with to help you learn a new language?

What are the best kinds of language learning materials?

What do they look like? Why do you think they're best?

What is good and not so good about the materials you are working with now? What do you think is missing from them?

What changes would you make to them?

....?

....?

....?

(Breen and Candlin 1987:27)

► TASK 28

Examine Low's list of potential participants (see Task 27) in the materials evaluation process and answer the following questions:

1 In what ways might the evaluation interests and questions of these individuals differ?

2 Why might they require different types of data and use different types of procedures when evaluating materials?

3 In the light of your understanding of the notions of formative and summative evaluation, identify those from the above list you think will be more interested in formative evaluation and those in summative evaluation.

It is important to recognize the different and relevant contributions to materials evaluation. As Low (1987:27) maintains: 'the evaluation of a language learning programme, or the materials used to teach it, involves more viewpoints than that of the 'independent' outside observer.'

Summary
In evaluating materials it is necessary to examine the ways in which teaching and learning materials are sensitive to the language learning process. Evaluation criteria should relate not only to the aims and contents of language learning, but also, and importantly, to the procedures for working with texts and performing tasks in the classroom. It is necessary to analyse learner outcomes, but not to the exclusion of evaluating other aspects of the teaching and learning process. From this we may conclude that a comprehensive evaluation of our teaching and learning materials will entail a theoretical (i.e. workplan) and empirical (i.e. process) analysis of materials, the data from which will be augmented with details of learner outcomes. The importance of observational data, derived from an analysis of materials in use, should not be undervalued.

Observation is also crucial to the evaluation of teachers and teaching, an issue to which we now turn.

2.5 Teachers and teaching

Purposes for classroom observation
Evaluation is a crucial part of teaching, but how is it done well? Testing knowledge of theory is not enough to judge effective teaching. We need to observe teachers in action using their knowledge in the real setting of the classroom. Classroom observation gives us the opportunity to see teachers putting theory into practice; it shows us what teachers *do* rather than what they know.

Grading teachers
Your own teaching context will influence your view on the purposes of classroom observation. The experience of many teachers suggests that it is primarily summative in purpose, inextricably bound up with reporting a grade, accountability, and judgemental statements.

▶ TASK 29

Consider the situation where a teacher-trainer on a pre-service course goes into a school to observe teaching practice with a checklist such as the following. To what extent is this list similar or dissimilar to ones used in a context you know? Give details.

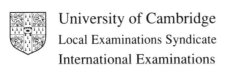 University of Cambridge
Local Examinations Syndicate
International Examinations

 EXAMINATION BOARD

DIPLOMA IN THE TEACHING OF ENGLISH AS A FOREIGN LANGUAGE TO ADULTS

CENTRE NUMBER					CANDIDATE NUMBER				

1st	2nd	College Assessment	Result

Final Examination Report on Practical Test

Candidate's Name				
Place of Examination			Date	
			Time	
Level of Class	Elementary	Previous contact with class	No. in class	
	Intermediate			
	Advanced			

Personal Qualities (See relevant Section in Handbook Nos. 1.1 to 1.6)	Strengths	Weaknesses
Comments	(Enter Ref. Nos.)	

Preparation (See relevant Section in Handbook Nos. 2.1 to 2.7)	Strengths	Weaknesses
Comments	(Enter Ref. Nos.)	

(Continues overleaf)

Execution (See relevant Section in Handbook Nos. 3 to 15.3)	Strengths	Weaknesses
Comments	(Enter Ref. Nos.)	

Summarising comments (including reference to Nos. 16 to 16.4)

Final Assessment	
Indicate: Distinction Pass or Fail	Examiner's Name and No.
	Signed

(RSA/UCLES 1988)

The focus when grading teachers using a checklist is mainly on the product of teaching and learning, for example, 'ability to establish rapport', 'suitability of materials and methods', 'use of aids'. Also, the checklist is used by an external observer. Typically, teachers are visited by inspectors who check their class records and lesson plans, observe a lesson, and then comment on the lessons using a checklist as a guide. Sometimes this evaluation is carried out without much participation by the teacher who is actually being observed.

▶ # TASK 30

In your context:

1 How are teachers observed? Give details.
2 Does the observation have a purpose other than grading teachers?
3 What role do you believe the observer should play when visiting teachers in schools?

Teacher development

Using observation merely to grade teachers, for example, with a view to promotion, is extremely limiting. It is important to use observation to provide information that teachers can use as a basis for future action. Here we refer to the formative value of classroom observation where the feedback from evaluation will be used to further develop or improve an aspect of classroom practice, or as part of curriculum betterment or teacher self-development. Consider this following way of evaluating teacher performance:

The classroom assessment process should consist of three stages:
1 pre-lesson material
2 the lesson
3 the trainee's post-lesson evaluation

1 The pre-lesson material includes:
  a information about the class: descriptive and evaluative
  b the scheme of work and the place of the assessed lesson in it
  c the lesson plan (normally accepted form)

2 The lesson; attention to the following:
  a classroom personality   d what is being sought
  b classroom management   e how it is being sought
  c awareness of learners   f what the learner is doing

The above should be gone into in detail.

3 Post-lesson evaluation; written self-assessment on:
  a the lesson plan
  b the major headings on the assessment schedule
  c any additional relevant points

(James 1983)

▶   TASK 31

1 Compare the checklist described earlier (pages 35–6) with the evaluation of the stages of teacher performance above.

2 How effective do you think these two different ways of observing are?

3 To what extent are the teachers involved in the observation and grading process?

In this second approach not only is the teacher formally included at stage 3 by means of a written self-assessment, but also there is an attempt to examine the process of teaching and learning. The category 'what the learner is doing' could highlight, for example, the nature of the interaction (teacher to learner, learner to learner, learner to teacher) or the type of writing that the learners are doing (copying from the blackboard, filling in a gapped passage, reordering words and sentences). An item on a checklist which focuses on 'how', i.e. what the teacher is doing, can also identify a wealth of information about the teacher and teaching, for example, 'What are the different question types that the teacher uses?' 'How are visual aids used at the different stages (presentation, practice, or production) of the lesson? Checklist items such as these focus attention on details of the teaching and learning process and provide information that is useful in terms of modifying and improving classroom practice. It is, therefore, an example of formative teaching evaluation.

Peer teaching is an alternative method of evaluating teachers in training. Here trainees 'teach' a lesson to their colleagues. Tutor and learner observers look out for specific points in the teaching practice. Feedback can come both from the trainer and fellow learners. Another way is using microteaching. In its simplest form a trainee teaches a group of learners for a short period of time, for example, fifteen minutes covering a specific topic or skill (apologizing, reading for specific information, etc.). Again, peers and/or a trainer observe this performance and comment on it using a checklist as a guide.

The observation involved in the above practices can be used for improving the teachers' techniques, monitoring their progress, and counselling them on relevant aspects of their teaching. However, in many cases, they are primarily geared towards training and grading, in other words, used to determine whether the training institution will qualify a teacher, the syllabus is being covered, the teacher uses the appropriate methodology, and so on. Additionally, not only is the observation largely controlled by someone other than the classroom teacher, but the checklist on p. 35–6 also reflects an external observer's judgement on what is effective teaching. There is a need to consider ways in which teachers themselves may become more involved in the process of evaluation.

Teacher self-development

A more participant-orientated evaluation through observation is important in raising teachers' awareness, a key feature of the teacher development process. Taking microteaching as an example, we can consider ways in which evaluation may be made more illuminative, collaborative, and useful in terms of teacher self-development. The process can be examined at three levels: self-evaluation, peer evaluation, and collaborative group work. We shall examine these in detail.

Teacher self-evaluation

Self-evaluation is simply the practice of teachers reflecting on what has taken place in the lesson with a view to improving their performance. It can be very informal, for example in the form of brief notes written immediately after the lesson. Or it can be part of a written (such as the class record) or oral report on the lesson itself. Alternatively, a checklist can be used. In the following example a teacher has completed a self-evaluation checklist about her relationships with her learners.

Section 2: Relationship with children   Personal comments

In relating to children, I am able to:

(a) Recognize and enhance the need in every child for a positive self-image   ⑤ I try!   ⑥

(b) Acknowledge and encourage children's ideas and contributions to activities.   ④ Too many children!   ④

(c) Interact with individual children every day.   ⑧   ⑧

(d) Thoroughly understand the personality needs of individuals and groups of children.   ⑤   ⑤

(e) Participate in activities alongside children.   ⑧   ⑧

(f) Understand when and when not to intervene in children's tasks.   ⑧   ⑧

(g) Communicate with children easily in verbal and non-verbal situations.   ④ Language 'problems' in this class / E2L   ⑤

(h) Recognize the growing influence of the peer group on children's attitudes and behaviour.   ③ Need to read up on this!   ③

(i) Be essentially positive and encouraging in all dealings with children.   ⑤   ⑤

(j) Provide a suitable adult 'model' for children.   ⑨   ⑨

(k) Make myself aware of child's background and other relevant information.   ⑥ Try hard! Can head help?   ⑤

(l) Use a variety of types of questioning to elicit thoughtful responses.   ② How can I ask more 'open' questions?   ②

(m) Make time to listen to children.   ⑤ As much as I can with 35!!   ⑥

(n) Recognize the need for awareness of equal opportunities for boys and girls.   ④ Cultural difficulties   ④

(o) Recognize the need for awareness of equal opportunities for children from all ethnic and cultural backgrounds.   ④ Many ethnic backgrounds to cope with   ④   5·3   15|80

Need to read up on open questioning + peer groups
See head re E2L children + backgrounds

1 → 2 → 3 → 4 → 5 → 6 → 7 → 8 → 9 → 10
Very inadequate   5·3   Excellent

(Moyles 1988:21)

In addition to indicating ratings on a scale 1 (Very inadequate) to 10 (Excellent), this teacher has added some personal comments. Although there is an average of 5.3 recorded, this score is not as important as the insights gained in a descriptive analysis of this kind. The following example of self-evaluation, reported in Nunan (1988:68), shows how the teaching of grammar can be monitored and evaluated.

Name: _____   Week of: _____

Class (language): _____   Level: _____   Period: _____

This is an inventory that asks you to identify how many times you used a given teaching practice in a particular class in a given week. Please use this key in responding to the following statements relating to different aspects of grammar presentations.

0 = Never   This is something I did not do in this particular class this week.
1 = Infrequently   This is something that I did once this week in the class.
2 = Sometimes   This is something I did two or three times a week in this class.
3 = Regularly   This is something that I did four or five times this week in this class.

In presenting a grammar teaching point for the first time I:

_____	1	Presented the teaching point both orally and with visual aids.
_____	2	Used pictures and diagrams to convey the meaning of the teaching point.
_____	3	Presented the teaching point indirectly in the context of spoken language, but did not formally teach it.
_____	4	Presented the teaching point indirectly in the context of written language, but did not formally teach it.
_____	5	Presented the teaching point indirectly in the context of spoken language and pointed it out to the students.
_____	6	Presented the teaching point indirectly in the context of written language and pointed it out to the students.
_____	7	Presented the teaching point using only the target language.
_____	8	Reviewed with the students relevant, previously presented grammatical structures.
_____	9	Gave the students several examples of the teaching point, and guided them in discovering the grammatical rule.
_____	10	Gave the students several examples of the teaching point, before supplying them with the grammatical rule.
_____	11	Translated examples of the teaching point to be certain that the students understood.
_____	12	Assisted the students in participating in a target-language conversation, then drew the teaching point from the language that the students themselves had generated.
_____	13	Spoke only in the target language, but modified the structure, vocabulary and speed so that the students could understand easily.
_____	14	Did not focus on grammar in the teaching of the language.
_____	15	Based new teaching points on previously presented grammatical structures.
_____	16	Gave only one example of the teaching point and did it orally.
_____	17	Embedded the teaching point in a command designed to elicit a non-verbal response from the students.
_____	18	Relied on gestures and mime to convey the meaning of the teaching point.
_____	19	Drew the teaching point from dialogues that the students had memorised.
_____	20	Explained the teaching point in English.
_____	21	Conducted oral drills on the teaching point before presenting it formally.
_____	22	Wrote the grammatical rule on the board/overhead before beginning to explain it.
_____	23	Gave the students the general grammatical rule, then wrote examples of the rule on the board/overhead.
_____	24	Allowed students to look at the explanation in their textbook while I was presenting the teaching point.
_____	25	Had the students read a grammar explanation in their texts before I presented it in class.

(Koziol and Call, cited in Nunan 1988)

Used over a period, this inventory will provide teachers with a fairly accurate record of the ways in which they approached the teaching of grammar. It will describe what they actually do as opposed to what they think they do.

► ## TASK 32

1 Think about the ways in which you correct learner errors. How do you correct them? When do you correct them? Do you always correct all errors?

2 Now draw up a self-evaluation checklist that you could use to detail the ways in which you manage error correction in your teaching.

One of the advantages of self-evaluation inventories of this kind is that they can be designed by individual teachers to suit their own teaching contexts. They are relatively simple to use and yet potentially they can provide a wealth of information about teachers, their teaching, and their learners.

Peer evaluation

Peer evaluation can be incorporated into microteaching where several trainees are present during the lesson or where they share the same microteaching session. Here it is important for there to be some means of encouraging open and constructively critical discussion.

► ## TASK 33

What kind of observation task would you suggest to encourage peer evaluation? How would it differ from the self-evaluation and external observer checklists shown above? Would you use a check-list at all?

Now, consider the following procedure (adapted from James 1983) which may involve both teacher self-evaluation and peer evaluation.

1 The teachers prepare an open profile of themselves as teachers. It is in the form of a sort of self-presentation which can precede the feedback session at the end of the microteaching.

2 Statements such as the following would make up a teacher's own professional principles:

I always correct learner errors.
I do not allow learners to use their first language.
I teach the rules of grammar to help learners use the language.
I never ask a learner to use language which has not been previously presented and practised.
I always use authentic materials as a basis for teaching.

I make certain that a large proportion of the learners' time is spent in group work.

I never ask learners to read aloud to the rest of the class.

I always mark learners' written work.

I believe that learner errors are the result of first language interference.

I try to exercise a strong personality in the classroom.

I adapt my teaching to suit what the learners say they want.

3 For each of these statements, the teachers in discussion groups indicate whether they agree or disagree. If there is disagreement then they are asked to rewrite the statement to reflect what they think.

▶ TASK 34

1 Do you agree with all the statements above? Rewrite the ones you disagree with or want to modify.

2 What other statements could you add to the above incomplete list which would be part of your general statement about your own practice in teaching?

Note the basic difference between this self-evaluation checklist and the more external-type checklist discussed at the beginning of this section (page 35); it does not presuppose any external observer. Nonetheless, in microteaching it can be used by both peers and tutors to discuss what constitutes elements of good teaching practice. Because peer evaluation is collaborative in approach, the teachers being observed might themselves suggest areas of their teaching that they feel need to be improved and ask their colleagues to concentrate on these.

At this point evaluation has moved away from the narrow summative functions of evaluation for grading purposes and has taken on illuminative and support functions and become formative in purpose.

Collaborative group work

This is a further extension of peer-evaluation where the focus of the evaluation is agreed on beforehand by the group. More control is in the hands of the peer group but it requires good leadership skills as outlined earlier (see 1.4). Collaborative group work can offer an additional opportunity to evaluate the trainer and the programme.

▶ TASK 35

1 Suggest ideas that a collaborative group observation could focus on. How would they implement these ideas?

2 Write down examples of the kind of questions you might ask learners in an evaluation of classroom practice.

Kouraogo (1987), in an article about Burkina Faso, discusses the function of teachers' self-help groups which can form the basis of a collaborative national teacher organisation.

▶ TASK 36

1 Can you think of ways in which self-help groups could be organized in your area?

2 How could they be organized? How many members in each group? How often would they meet?

3 Could the discussions feed into a national organization? When could a national meeting be arranged?

Kouraogo suggests that groups could meet on a monthly basis and discuss the practical problems that teachers have. At a later date, these small groups and their discussion topics could be brought together in a national conference. One of the purposes of these self-help groups is that they may not only help teachers resolve practical problems, but may also encourage and support teachers in difficult circumstances.

Summary
We have moved from the narrow perspective of grading teacher performance to an evaluation of teachers and teaching which can provide information of practical use to teachers for the development of their teaching. Evaluation through observation is useful at all stages of a teacher's career to improve the quality of teaching for the benefit of the learners. It may be a gradual process which is initially prompted by an external observer but later moves towards self-evaluation. Since teachers may find themselves in a situation where there is little or no in-service training, evaluation can be the means to understanding their own teaching better, improving their performance, and adapting to the changing needs of the classroom. Evaluation in this broad sense is an important part of teacher education which teachers can use throughout their careers.

2.6 Evaluating learner outcomes

When we test learners there are a number of decisions that as teachers we need to take, for example when to test, which type of test to use, and how we are going to mark this test. Evaluation at the different stages in the testing process can help us make appropriate decisions about classroom testing. Below we look at the different stages through which teachers need to progress in order to select or construct the appropriate assessment procedure for classroom use. We start (where much discussion usually ends) by exploring the nature of feedback that can be obtained from our tests and then using this information as the central organizing principle on which the evaluations are based.

Stage 1: Feedback from tests
Qualitative or quantitative feedback?

The first decision to make is whether we want quantitative or qualitative feedback from the tests.

▶ **TASK 37**

Think of the tests (formal and informal) used in your context.

1 Why do your learners take them?

2 Describe the kind of feedback that they provide:
   a) for the teacher
   b) for the learners
   c) for anyone else

Much current classroom practice involves the reporting of test results using a number or grade. This quantitative record of learner performance is of little use to the classroom teacher. If a learner continually hovers around the pass/fail borderline whenever tested, the actual mark of $4\frac{1}{2}$ out of 10 (assuming that 5 constitutes a pass mark), or forty-nine percent, does not provide any guidance as to what this learner must do to improve performance. What would be more helpful to this learner is to know why marks were awarded on the test (what was good and adequate) and why marks were not given (where the test performance failed to reach an acceptable pass level).

The extract opposite is a profile of learner performance from the Primary Language Record (Barrs et al., 1988:51). It shows the teacher's comments about a child's retelling of a traditional story and notes the significance of this in the child's development as a writer.

Profiles of this type, providing qualitative statements about learner outcomes, are more likely to be meaningful and of some future use to teachers and learners than numerical scores.

Delayed or immediate feedback?
Sometimes learners receive feedback soon after taking a test; at other times the results are delayed. If we want to make good and appropriate use of feedback, the sooner both learners and teachers have access to feedback the better so that teacher intervention and learner action can be planned.

Delays in marking tests can often be explained by pressures of work on individual teachers. There is, therefore, a strong case for considering ways in which teachers' marking loads can be appropriately reduced.

The type of test will influence the amount of time spent on marking. Essay-type tests are notoriously time-consuming to mark; more guided writing tasks less so. Also, teachers can involve learners in the assessment process such that feedback from a learning task can be obtained during a

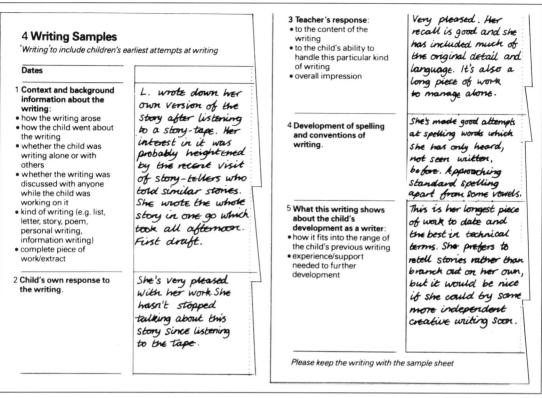

4 Writing Samples

'Writing' to include children's earliest attempts at writing

Dates

1 **Context and background information about the writing:**
- how the writing arose
- how the child went about the writing
- whether the child was writing alone or with others
- whether the writing was discussed with anyone while the child was working on it
- kind of writing (e.g. list, letter, story, poem, personal writing, information writing)
- complete piece of work/extract

L. wrote down her own version of the story after listening to a story-tape. Her interest in it was probably heightened by the recent visit of story-tellers who told similar stories. She wrote the whole story in one go which took all afternoon. First draft.

2 **Child's own response to the writing.**

She's very pleased with her work. She hasn't stopped talking about this story since listening to the tape.

3 **Teacher's response:**
- to the content of the writing
- to the child's ability to handle this particular kind of writing
- overall impression

Very pleased. Her recall is good and she has included much of the original detail and language. It's also a long piece of work to manage alone.

4 **Development of spelling and conventions of writing.**

She's made good attempts at spelling words which she has only heard, not seen written, before. Approaching standard spelling apart from some vowels.

5 **What this writing shows about the child's development as a writer:**
- how it fits into the range of the child's previous writing
- experience/support needed to further development

This is her longest piece of work to date and the best in technical terms. She prefers to retell stories rather than branch out on her own, but it would be nice if she could try some more independent creative writing soon.

Please keep the writing with the sample sheet

(Barrs et al. 1988:51)

lesson. Peer appraisal can focus on different aspects of language use, for example, the use of correct question forms, the number of content points made, or the range of vocabulary items. Alternatively, in a reading lesson learners can devise their own questions for each other and act as monitors of responses.

▶ TASK 38

Think of a learning task. How could a teacher organize this task so that the learners provide feedback for each other and for the teacher?

It is important for teachers to explore ways in which (1) tests can be marked more easily, and (2) learners can become more involved in the testing process. The advantage of learner involvement is that the feedback is both immediate and qualitative. Course appraisal is largely formative, pedagogic, diagnostic, and process-oriented where outcomes will be qualitative and descriptive. This contrasts with summative tests that grade learners, where the tests are formal, largely external to teaching and learning, and product-oriented.

▶ TASK 39

How would you describe the ways learners are tested in your context? Identify the formative and summative elements in these tests.

The distinctions raised above allow us to state two fundamental purposes to feedback. These are summarized in Figure 4 below.

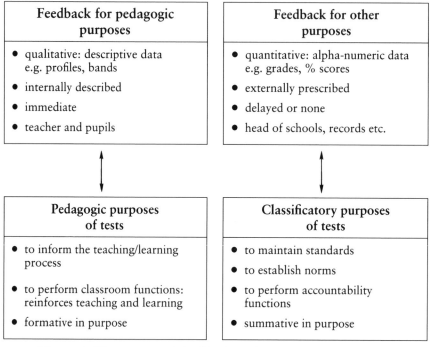

Feedback for pedagogic purposes	**Feedback for other purposes**
• qualitative: descriptive data e.g. profiles, bands	• quantitative: alpha-numeric data e.g. grades, % scores
• internally described	• externally prescribed
• immediate	• delayed or none
• teacher and pupils	• head of schools, records etc.

Pedagogic purposes of tests	**Classificatory purposes of tests**
• to inform the teaching/learning process	• to maintain standards
• to perform classroom functions: reinforces teaching and learning	• to establish norms
	• to perform accountability functions
• formative in purpose	• summative in purpose

Figure 4 *The nature of feedback and test purpose*
(Rea-Dickins 1989)

It can be seen from Figure 4 that the type of feedback wanted will influence the kind of test used. Once the type of feedback you need is identified, you can evaluate the primary purpose of your testing procedures. If, for example, you decide that your purpose for testing is pedagogic, you would expect your feedback to share most of the characteristics listed in the top left hand box of Figure 4. However, if your test has given results in terms of percentages, then clearly your pedagogic purpose for testing and the feedback (in this case 'classificatory') differ. Evaluation of feedback is very important both for your teaching and for your learners.

Having evaluated in Stage 1 (as illustrated by Figure 4) the precise purpose for testing, the selection of your test type follows.

Stage 2: Test type

Classification

If your purpose is to categorize learners in some way, this will influence the type of test you select. A *placement* test serves the purpose of placing learners in a class at the appropriate level. If, on the other hand, you need to make a selection from a large number of learners for entry to a specific course, then a *selection* or *screening* test is needed. In both cases your main objective is to classify learners. In order to do this, your test needs to be able to discriminate between learners at the appropriate level. To the extent that the test content may be based on a specific syllabus, or textbook, your test type will also share the characteristics of an *attainment* or *achievement* test.

Where your test is not linked to any specific syllabus or course and relates to external target performance levels, the test type you select will be a *proficiency* test. Notable examples of proficiency tests are the IELTS (British Council/UCLES) and the TOEFL (Educational Testing Service). Such tests may well be administered at the end of a teaching programme, and not be in any direct way integrated within a teaching and learning situation.

Pedagogic

Alternatively, when you want input for teaching purposes, you need a test to guide you in the principled monitoring of learner progress. This means that the test should provide specific information in the form of descriptive statements with which you can plan for the next stage of teaching or for a classroom change of some kind. This implies that the test be related to the aims of your particular syllabus, specifically to units of work that have been covered in class. The test type will be an *achievement* or *attainment* test, and if the test is designed to assess specific or discrete aspects of the learning programme, it may also have a *diagnostic* dimension.

▶ **TASK 40**

1 Think of a test you are familiar with.
   a) What type of test is this?
   b) What kind of feedback does it provide?
   c) Does it achieve what it is supposed to do?
2 Of the test types described above, which do you think will provide the most useful information for teaching purposes?

Summary

The type of test you administer is determined by your overall purpose for testing which, in turn, has been influenced by the kind of information required from a test. This brings us to the third stage that teachers need to evaluate in the classroom testing process.

Stage 3: Test strategy
When evaluating which test to use, two issues need to be considered.

Whose responsibility?
The first issue concerns where and/or with whom the responsibility for the testing rests. Traditionally this has been considered the teachers' domain, or that of an institution or governmental body, but does this need to be the case? Does the teacher, or institution, have to play the predominant role? As indicated earlier, there is a role for peer involvement in the testing process. The issue of 'control over' the test hinges on, minimally, three things: the function of the test, the nature of the feedback required, and the receiver of the information from the test.

Where the test function is external to teaching and learning, with outcomes specified in percentage scores or grades, there is less of a case for, and acceptance of, 'learner control'. The reverse becomes true where the test function is as 'informant' to the teaching process, that is where testing is integral to teaching and learning.

Test procedure
The second issue concerns the kind of test used. Traditional practice favours pencil and paper tests but tests can take other forms. This may entail a shift of responsibility from the teacher to the learner. Other procedures include learner self-reports (for example self-appraisal, diary or record keeping—see Oskarsson 1978, Lewkowicz and Moon 1985, Murphy-O'Dwyer 1985, and Brindley 1989), the building of profiles of abilities negotiated between learner and teacher, the use of interactive video, computer-aided testing, and peer appraisal. With reference to learner involvement, Lewkowicz and Moon recognize that testing:

'should not be seen as a one-way process in which learners are judged by a teacher or outside body on the basis of externally defined criteria; it must be seen as a multi-way dynamic system in which learners are involved interactively with others in making judgements about themselves both as learners and users of the language on the basis of criteria which are defined and negotiated in terms of the learning situation.'
(Lewkowicz and Moon 1985:47)

▶ TASK 41

> Give an example that would work in your class where learners could be involved in the appraisal of written work.

Consider the situation in which a writing test has been administered to a class. The teacher collects the responses and makes a careful selection of between four and six of them. Learners then work in pairs, or small groups, and judge the quality of the different answers that have been circulated. This has the advantage that the marking criteria will be made clear to the learners. (How often is it the case that learners are unaware of how marks are assigned on tests?) It also encourages the development of a critical approach to written work so that learners may be better able to edit their own work.

► TASK 42

1 Give reasons for and/or against peer appraisal in your classroom contexts.
2 Does this depend on the type of test administered and who requires the information from the test?

The benefit of peer appraisal is that it provides increased learner participation in, and shared responsibility for, classroom learning than conventional paper and pencil tests. Typically one talks in terms of teachers as monitors of learners' performance, but there is no reason why learners cannot themselves take part in this monitoring process. Indeed, it is argued here that this participation is advantageous for classroom testing where the information from the test(s) becomes an integral part of the teaching and learning.

Once you have decided on the procedures you wish to adopt, then you will need to evaluate what content you are going to test. This brings us to the fourth stage in the testing process.

Stage 4: Test content
Teachers are faced with two principal questions about test content: 'How do I evaluate "what" is to be tested?' and 'How much should be tested?'

Precise test content specifications depend on factors relating to the interaction between your purpose for giving a test and the timing of the test within the teaching programme, as we now explain.

There are at least two ways of evaluating the role of testing during the course of teaching. First, when a test relates back to an immediately preceding lesson or unit of work, it is more likely to have a very specific focus and narrow coverage of course content, such as a task on greetings, the active and passive voice, or reading for specific information. Second, when the purpose is to review a variety of material, taught over a longer time scale, test content will involve a wider coverage of items and have a more general focus. Consider Figure 5 below.

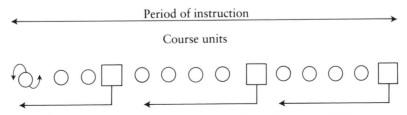

Figure 5 *Test content and test timing (Rea-Dickins 1989)*

The circles refer to tests with a very selective focus, that refer to immediate classroom content such as the use of *can/be able/could* to express ability, possibility, asking for permission. As suggested by Figure 5, these appraisal points are more frequent in classroom use (an individual teacher will determine the precise number), and it is also likely that they will involve only one test activity. These formative tests are contrasted with those identified by a square, which are administered less frequently and have a more global focus and wider coverage of content because they refer back to a series of lessons within a programme of instruction. Additionally, a range of activities may be used to ensure adequate content coverage; and there will be greater emphasis on the assessment of integrated skills.

Sometimes revision units in textbooks take the form of tests.

▶ TASK 43

Analyse the three tests opposite which are extracts from Review Unit 3 (62–63) of Black et al. (1988), *Fast Forward 2* (Resource Book) with reference to points made about informal class testing. Some questions are provided to guide you.

1 What kind of feedback will the test provide? (quantitative? qualitative?)

2 How could the results be reported to the learners? In what way could these results help the learners?

3 How could the results be used by the teacher?

4 What type of test is it?

5 How easy are these tests to mark? Make suggestions as to how these tests could be marked. By whom? To what extent could the learners be involved in this process?

6 What content is being tested? Do you think the focus is selective or general?

7 Do you think it is a formative or a summative test?

As far as classroom testing is concerned, that is, when the purpose for testing has been identified as pedagogic, the focus of tests can be both selective and general, with a predominance of content-focused activities. In contrast to this, when testing has a classificatory purpose (see Figure 4), a general and global content focus is more relevant.

The fifth stage in the testing process is affected by the extent to which a test has either a narrow and selective focus or a broader and more global one. It involves an evaluation of the appropriate criteria for marking a test. This is considered next.

Stage 5: Marking criteria
Teachers should know in advance of administering a test which marking criteria they will use to mark learners' work.

1 Use the gerund or infinitive (with *to*) form of the verbs in brackets.

1 **Tom** I really fancy (go) _____ out

today. Maybe I'll go (sail) _____

I've been longing (go) _____

sailing for ages.

Bill I wouldn't do that if I were you. It's too

windy.

Tom Maybe you're right but I don't think I ought

(stay) _____ at home on such a

lovely day.

Bill Why don't you just sunbathe instead? I'll be

worried.

Tom OK, I won't go (sail) _____.

I promise I'll lie on the beach.

Tom felt like (go) _____ sailing, but his friend

advised him to avoid (go) _____ as it was

too windy. He suggested (sunbathe) _____

instead. Tom agreed (not go) _____ sailing

and promised (stay) _____ on the beach.

2 Fill the spaces with one of these words:

however anyone whenever no one whoever
everyone whatever someone wherever whoever
something whom

LOST PROPERTY

To .... it may concern.

.... we receive lost property,

.... it is found, we take it to the

caretaker's office and keep it for two

months. .... claims the property

is asked to donate .... to charity,

.... small; but sometimes

.... comes forward. At the end

of the year, ... lost property

we have left is sold, ... it

belongs to, and the proceeds go to charity.

.... agrees that this is a good

way of raising funds. This year we need

.... to help at the jumble sale.

Is .... free next Saturday? Please

contact the Chief Steward, Room 19A.

3 Match the announcements with a suitable reply from below. Fill the spaces in the replies with these words and phrases:

your help meeting you attend your party sympathy
your new baby your good wishes

1 Janet and Terry Smith are pleased
to announce the birth of
Jacqueline Alice
on May 23rd at Thames Hospital,
weighing 7.2 kilos.

2 *In Memoriam*
Mr David Richards, loving husband of
Janette and beloved father of Joe and
Kate, died peacefully at St Lawrence
Hospital on Monday.

3 Mr and Mrs Hamilton request the
pleasure of your company on the
occasion of their daughter's 21st
birthday, on 5th March at Woodland
Manor, Lincoln Gardens, from 8 pm to
1 am.
R.S.V.P.

4 BON VOYAGE !
GOOD LUCK IN YOUR NEW JOB

5 The bank has therefore agreed to
the £20,000 loan you requested in
order to expand your business.

6 PLANE ARRIVES HEATHROW 6.30 PM
FLIGHT BA273 PLEASE MEET

... I regret that I was unable to ......

.... I look forward to ....

...... Please accept our heartfelt ....

.... I was delighted to hear
about ....

I am most grateful for ....

Thank you for ....

(Black et al. 1988a:63)

▶   TASK 44

Examine these marking criteria:

Grammar	Organization	Style	Fluency
Vocabulary	Cohesion	Relevance	Tenses
Appropriateness	Content	Accuracy	Effort

1 Which of these criteria are used in tests, formal and informal, you are familiar with?

2 Make a list of other criteria used that do not appear in the list.

For class tests, most teachers look to the syllabus and textbook as the main source of their marking criteria. These criteria are usually of two kinds. The first includes all those criteria that focus on accuracy of language use, such as grammar, vocabulary, pronunciation, intonation, and stress. The second has been underscored by communicative approaches to language teaching and includes criteria such as style, appropriateness, organization, ability to get message across, amount of communication, effort to communicate, fluency, relevance of content. The point is that if you know what is being tested then you should also know how, i.e. by which criteria, this content is to be assessed.

▶   TASK 45

Think of the marking criteria used in tests you are familiar with.

1 Do the learners who sit these tests also know the criteria used?

2 Do these vary according to the type of test used?

3 How much do your learners know about how their work is marked?

When you take driving lessons, you are aware of the criteria your instructor is using to help you improve on your performance. You may be advised to reduce your speed when approaching traffic lights or to keep nearer the kerb. By the same token, when your learners are using language, they should be aware of how their performances are being appraised. In an oral test, for example, are they being assessed on their language production only, or are they also being graded on their comprehension of what is said to them? If learners are unaware of the criteria used, how can they take steps to improve their performances?

When you have selected the appropriate marking criteria, you then have to decide on which marking scheme to use, because marking criteria can be applied in a variety of ways. There are three main approaches.

Impressionistic marking schemes
This approach is where marks are awarded on the basis of a teacher's overall impression. In contrast with the analytic marking scheme, credit is

not given for specific categories and a learner's performance is expressed as a single mark or grade. This is sometimes referred to as *holistic* or *subjective* marking. In an attempt to improve the reliability of impressionistic marking, analytic marking and profiling is increasingly used.

Analytic marking schemes
The analytic approach to marking has the advantage of providing diagnostic detail of use to both teachers and learners. Here is an example:

Content	5 marks	Structure	5 marks
Organization	5 marks	Spelling, Punctuation	5 marks

Profiles
These describe learner performance at a range of different levels and in different areas, as the following general training module profile from IELTS (1990) shows. It uses six bands, or levels, to describe learner outcomes on a writing task. (The band descriptions below were in use at the time of going to press, but are under constant review.)

	Coherence and cohesion	Word choice, form and spelling	Sentence structure
6 or above.	The message can be followed throughout. Information is generally arranged coherently but cohesion within and/or between sentences may be faulty with misuse, overuse or omission of cohesive devices.	The range of vocabulary sometimes appears limited as does the appropriacy of its use. Minor limitations of, or errors in, word choice sometimes intrude on the reader. Word formation and spelling errors occur but are only slightly intrusive.	Sentence structures are generally adequate, but the reader may feel that control is achieved by the use of a restricted range of structures or, in contrast, that the use of a wide variety of structures is not marked by the same level of structural accuracy.
5	The message can generally be followed although sometimes only with difficulty. Both coherence and cohesion may be faulty.	The range of vocabulary and the appropriacy of its use are limited. Lexical confusion and incorrect word choice are noticeable. Word formation and spelling errors may be quite intrusive.	There is a limited range of sentence structures and the greatest accuracy is achieved on short, simple sentences. Errors in such areas as agreement of tenses or subjects and verbs are noticeable.
4	The message is difficult to follow. Information is not arranged coherently, and cohesive devices are inadequate or missing.	The range of vocabulary is often inadequate and/or inappropriate. Word choice causes serious problems for the reader. Word formation and spelling errors cause severe strain for the reader.	Limited control of sentence structures, even short simple ones, is evident. Errors in such areas as agreement of tenses or of subjects and verbs cause severe strain for the reader.
3	The message cannot be followed. Neither coherence nor cohesion are apparent.	The reader is aware of gross inadequacies of vocabulary, word forms and spelling.	Control of sentence structure is evident only occasionally and errors predominate.
2	There is no recognizable message.	The reader sees no control of word choice, word forms and spelling.	There is little or no evidence of control of sentence structure.
1	Virtual non-writer.	Virtual non-writer.	Virtual non-writer.
0	Should only be used where a candidate did not attend or did not attempt this question in any way.		

(IELTS Assessment Guide to the Writing Test, UCLES 1990)

Summative profiles focus on the end product of teaching whereas *formative profiles* are an ongoing attempt to describe learners' abilities. In both cases, there is little emphasis on giving marks. Instead, learner attention is drawn to those categories which have been satisfactorily fulfilled and those where further improvement is required. In this way, learners can be encouraged not to compete with each other and compare marks, but to focus on the descriptive feedback provided by the activity.

▶ TASK 46

Compare the profile on page 45 with the one on page 53. Which do you think provides a formative description and which one a summative statement of learner outcomes? Explain why.

A further advantage of profile reporting is that the classroom teacher has enormous flexibility in describing performance levels. They can also provide clear descriptions of performance across the whole range of language and skills areas that are taught.

▶ TASK 47

Consider the types of marking schemes used in your teaching contexts.
1 Which ones are used: impressionistic, analytic, or profiles?
2 Does the type of marking scheme used vary with the type of test administered?
3 Which of the three marking schemes presented above do you think provides the most information?

Marking criteria are not selected on a whim. Criteria such as accuracy in the use of grammar, vocabulary, and pronunciation have traditionally been used for marking. Within the context of communicative teaching, however, other criteria are equally relevant. The decision that the teacher, in co-operation with the learners, has to make concerns an appropriate selection from the range of potential criteria. Appropriateness is determined according to the focus and the purpose of the testing activity in relation to classroom teaching. Further, teachers should have reasons for selecting a particular marking scheme. There is a place in the classroom context for both analytic schemes and profiles. Impressionistic marking is the least useful because it provides little formative information as the basis for teacher or learner action. These points lead naturally to the final evaluation point for the classroom teacher, that of selecting the appropriate test.

Stage 6: Test selection
Deciding on the best test to use becomes straightforward once you have evaluated each of the requirements at the various stages examined in this section. These are summarized as follows:

Stage 1: Determine nature of the feedback from tests
Stage 2: Determine test type
Stage 3: Determine test strategy
Stage 4: Determine test content

Stage 5: Determine marking criteria and marking scheme
Stage 6: Select/write appropriate test

▶   TASK 48

Imagine you want to give your learners a test. Follow the summary
above and record the decisions you make at each stage. Then suggest a suitable test to match your requirements.

Summary
Six main stages in the testing process have been examined which teachers
need to evaluate in order to select an appropriate test. In line with the rest
of this book, testing is approached from the aspect of testing used as a
tool to inform the teaching and learning process. The novelty here is that
the starting point is the nature of feedback and this is then used to
influence all the other stages in the process of selecting an appropriate
test. Thus instead of starting with the tests themselves, we have used the
nature of feedback as the central criterion on which classroom testing
practices should be based. Specifically, we have argued for formative tests
as an integral part of normal classwork because they reinforce both teaching and learning.

2.7 Summary

We have seen that there are three principal reasons for conducting an
evaluation. The first is for assessment and accountability where the information obtained can be used primarily for administrative purposes. In the
second and third, evaluation can serve a developmental function where it
can be used for purposes of curriculum development on the one hand and
teacher self-development on the other.

We have also examined the distinction between formative and summative
evaluation, where formative enquiries are concerned mainly with gathering data over time with a view to raising awareness and, through decisions made by teachers at a local level, bringing about improvements of
classroom practice. They are essentially developmental in their focus.
Summative evaluation, on the other hand, gives rise to evaluative judgements for purposes of decision making at project, institutional, or
national levels. As such they are more likely to focus on outcomes at the
end of a period of instruction rather than aspects of the process of teaching and learning.

An evaluation may focus on a variety of different parts of the language
teaching curriculum. In the first two sections, the principles of evaluation
were highlighted with reference to learning materials, teachers, teaching,
and learners. When the subject for evaluation is known, it is then necessary to select appropriate evaluation procedures. The different ways of
carrying out evaluations are considered next.

3 How can teachers evaluate their classrooms?

3.1 Introduction

Earlier (see **2.2**) a distinction was drawn between descriptive data-based and measurement-based evaluations. As an example, it was seen in the consideration of learner assessment (**2.6**) that profiles and learner self reports provide descriptive data, whereas tests provide measurement-based data. We examine first a measurement approach to evaluation.

3.2 Measurement-based evaluation

Several course evaluations have adopted a measurement approach. Allwright (1988) describes one such study. He reports the work of Scherer and Wertheimer (1964) who were interested in evaluating the relative superiority of two methods of teaching: the 'audiolingual' method and the 'traditional' method. Their study was primarily designed with the aim of proving that new methods are better than old ones. Working with groups of learners at university level, they compared a control group taught by the traditional method with an experimental group who were exposed to the then new audiolingual approach to language teaching. Their evaluation was designed as follows:

Evaluation aims
To compare two different methods of teaching: the audiolingual and the traditional method.

Experimental design
Two groups of learners kept separate over a two year period:

1 Control Group: no change in the type of instruction received, i.e. continued with the 'traditional' instructional method.
2 Experimental Group: taught by the new method, i.e. according to the principles of the audiolingual instructional method.

Evaluation procedures
Language tests administered to both control and experimental groups at the end of the period of instruction, i.e. after two years.

Results
Interpreted on basis of learners' test results, and expressed in terms of whether a statistically significant result was obtained.

This study is typical of many evaluation studies:

1 It is measurement-based: results were evaluated on the basis of test results.
2 It is summative: the evaluation focused on the end product of the course as measured by learner performance on tests set after two years.
3 It is deductive in approach: it sets out with a theory or hypothesis to prove.

The stages in this style of evaluation procedure can be summarized in the following manner.

Step 1: Establish a hypothesis
First establish a hypothesis which is a deduction from theory and then set out to *test* this predetermined theory. The hypothesis for this study was that one method, namely the audiolingual method, was superior to another, namely the traditional method.

Step 2: Select identical groups
Identify an experimental group who will receive the 'treatment' condition, and a control group which does not receive the treatment. In this study the experimental group was taught by the audiolingual approach; the control group received instruction according to traditional principles.

Step 3: Test the hypothesis or theory
In the majority of cases, as with the Scherer and Wertheimer (1964) study described above, a post-test is administered to both experimental and control groups.

Step 4: Interpretation of results
Statistically calculate the differences in the test results between the experimental and control groups. Interpret the results in the light of quantitative, i.e. statistical information.

Another study that set out to evaluate different methods of foreign language teaching, the Pennsylvania Project (Clark 1969), adopted a similar 'theory-driven', deductive approach. Additionally, however, it attempted (rather unsuccessfully) to gather data from the classroom situation, thereby recognizing the importance of 'data-based', inductive procedures in the evaluation process. The purpose of the observational component was to determine whether there existed in practice a real difference between the three instructional methods identified. Classrooms can be labelled 'audiolingual', 'traditional', or 'communicative', but what goes on in these classes may not reflect the labels assigned to them. For example, so-called communicative materials could be taught in a very traditional way. And without an observational component to the evaluation, it may never be discovered that classroom practice actually differs from the theoretical label assigned to a class. Examples of systematic classroom observation are provided in **6.4–6, 7.3, 8.3**, and **14.4**.

In order to examine alternatives to deductive measurement-driven approaches, descriptive data-based evaluation procedures are considered next.

3.3 Descriptive data-based evaluation

We have just examined an approach typically used for formal, summative evaluations. However, this type of evaluation does not provide the ELT practitioner with the kind of information that is useful in the forward planning of work. There are other procedures that incorporate a formative element by evaluating aspects of the ELT curriculum in progress. They seek to provide the teacher with insights into what is actually happening when teaching and learning is taking place.

The main procedures considered here for collecting data as the basis for evaluations are self-assessment forms, questionnaires, observation, checklists and inventories, and diaries.

Self-assessment forms

Student self-assessment is used as part of the formative evaluation of the Council of Europe European Young Workers and Youth Leaders course that is run annually at Ealing College London (now the Polytechnic of West London). At the end of every week, learners complete a self-evaluation form which is handed in to their Course Director. Here is an example:

Council of Europe: Name: _____

European Young Workers   Course: _____

European Youth Leaders   Week: _____

SELF-EVALUATION

To be completed by each student at the end of every week and handed in to your Course Director on the following Monday morning.

1 **Out-of-class practice**
   How much time outside class have you spent: Approx hours

          Speaking English?   _____

          Listening to English?   _____

          Reading English?   _____

          Writing English?   _____

2 Who have you spoken to this week in English? (not including your teacher)

          e.g. other course members _____

          members of the public _____

          other _____

Do you feel your conversations were generally successful?　Yes/No
Why? ————————————————————————————

3　What films/TV programmes/radio programmes have you seen/listened to this week? ——————————————————————————
————————————————————————————————
————————————————————————————————

What did you think of it? ————————————————————
Did it help you with your English? ————————————————
If yes, how? ————————————————————————————
If no, why not? ————————————————————————

4　What did you read in English this week?
————————————————————————————————
————————————————————————————————
————————————————————————————————

What did you think of it? ————————————————————
Did it help you with your English? ————————————————
If yes, how? ————————————————————————————
If no, why not? ————————————————————————

5　Have you written anything in English this week?
If yes, what? ——————————————————————————

6　Write down 10 new words in English you have learnt this week with their translation in your language.

translation

————————————————　　————————————————
————————————————　　————————————————
————————————————　　————————————————
————————————————　　————————————————
————————————————　　————————————————
————————————————　　————————————————
————————————————　　————————————————
————————————————　　————————————————
————————————————　　————————————————
————————————————　　————————————————

Where did you learn these?
Class　　　　　　　——————————————————————
Other (please specify)　——————————————————

7　**General progress**
What progress do you feel you have made in English this week?

	a lot	quite a lot	a little	not at all
speaking	———	————	———	————
listening	———	————	———	————
reading	———	————	———	————
writing	———	————	———	————

(Continues overleaf)

> 8 What are you going to work on/try to improve next week?
>   speaking   _____
>   listening _____
>   reading   _____
>   writing   _____
>   How are you going to do this? _____
>   _____
>   _____
>   _____
>
> 9 Now rate your progress for this week on your own personal scale from
>   1–10.
>   (1 = lowest 10 = highest)
>   1   2   3   4   5   6   7   8   9   10

(Miletto 1990)

The advantage of this approach is that learners benefit from keeping an ongoing record of their learning and responses to the programme of instruction. Their teachers can adjust the programme according to this information.

Checklists and inventories
Checklists are also very flexible and straightforward to design. You have already seen an example for the teaching of grammar (page 37); similar checklists can be constructed to provide data about other teaching and learning events. The following checklist, adapted from Ellis (1989), is one that teachers can use to describe how they administer class tests.

A feedback observation form

Stage	What the teacher did or said	Suggestions
1 Initial explanation		
....	....	....
2 Giving back students' answer sheets		
....	....	....
3 Explaining the marking scheme		
....	....	....
4 Commenting on the students' answers		
....	....	....
5 Instructing students to rewrite		
....	....	....
6 Dealing with student enquiries		
....	....	....

(after Ellis 1989)

The principal advantage of data-gathering procedures, such as question-naires and checklists, is that the feedback they provide can be used to make adjustments to aspects of teaching and learning. They may provide either quantitative data or qualitative data, as in the student self-evalua-tion questionnaire and in the teacher self-report checklist.

Diaries

Information obtained through diaries is not predetermined (by the question or the checklist) since it is the diarist, for example the teacher, colleague, or learner, who determines what is to be written. In particular, learners' diaries provide an interesting learner perspective on classroom practices. Consider the following diary:

23-9-88

Terribly disappointed with the language learning skills that I supposedly have. Thought it was a mistake to have taken up German but a few hours later on train had a look at the book and understood a bit more. My listening skills have never been good at all and teacher didn't want me to have a look at my book. However I learned to introduce myself and ask someone else's name. I also learned to spell my name which I found relatively easy. I hadn't been a school language st. for a few years therefore I felt that my pride was being bashed a bit. The whole experience was a shock to the system basically, long words with lots of consonants in them.

24-9

I feel slightly better as I am beginning to master a few sounds. The numbers seem to be a 'pain'. Teacher (one of them) seems to be unable to focus on one grammatical point, she does bits here and bits there; pretty confusing.

(Ellis and Rathbone 1988)

▶ TASK 49

1 From this learner's diary, what can you say about his/her attitudes to learning a foreign language?

2 If he/she were a learner of yours, how would his/her comments influence your teaching?

Observation

▶ TASK 50

You have been asked to evaluate two courses, one communicative and the other structural. You intend to evaluate whether those classes called 'communicative' actually are communicative and whether those labelled 'structural' display the principles of the structural approach to language teaching.

Make a list of some of the features you would expect to observe in (1) the communicative classroom and (2) the structural lesson.

Spada (1987) used the COLT (Communicative Observation of Language Teaching) observation scheme to analyse the communicative orientation of several classes for English as a second language.

School Teacher Subject	Grade(s) Lesson (Minutes)	Date Observer

Col. 1   2   3 4 5 6 7 8 9 10 11 12 13 14 15 16 17 18 19 20 21 22 23 24 25 26 27 28 29 30 31 32 33 34 35 36 37 38 39 40 41 42 43 44 45 46 47 48

Time	Activities	Partic Organization				Content				Student		Materials	
		Class	Group	Comb	Man.	Language	Other Topics		Topic Control	Modality		Type	Use

Narrow — Limited — Broad

Key codes (column headers):
T–S/C, S–S/C, Choral, Different, Same, Individual, Gr/Ind, Procedure, Discipline, Form, Function, Discourse, Socioling, Classroom, Stereotyp, Pers./Bio, Other, Personal, Rout./Soc, Fam./Com, School T, Other, Abstract, Pers./Ref., Imagination, World T, Other, Teacher, Teacher/Stud, Student, Listening, Speaking, Reading, Writing, Other, Minimal — Extended, Audio, Visual, Pedagogic, Semi-Pedag, Non-Pedag, High Control, Semi Control, Mini Control

KEY	Partic.	= participant	Ind.	= individual	Rout./Soc.	= routine/social
	T–S/C	= teacher to student/class	MAN.	= management	Fam./Com.	= family/community
	S–S/C	= student to student/class	Socioling.	= sociolinguistic	School T.	= school topic
	Comb.	= combination	Stereotyp.	= stereotypical	Pers./Ref.	= personal/referential
	Gr.	= group	Pers./Bio.	= personal/biographical	World T.	= world topic

(Spada 1987)

This part of the observation schedule focuses on the communicative features of teacher and learner verbal exchanges. Spada explains the section of Information Gap activities as follows:

II Information gap

This feature refers to the extent to which the information requested and/or exchanged is unpredictable, i.e., not known in advance.

A Requesting information
   1 Pseudo (The Speaker already possesses the information requested.)
   2 Genuine (The information requested is not known in advance.)

B Giving information
   1 Relatively predictable (The message is easily anticipated in that there is a very limited range of information that can be given. In the case of responses, only one answer is possible semantically, although there may be different correct grammatical realizations.)
   2 Relatively unpredictable (The message is not easily anticipated in that a wide range of information can be given. If a number of responses are possible, each can provide different information.)

(*Fröhlich et al. 1985*)

Alternatively, if you were to analyse the extent to which specific errors were corrected in the classroom, you might use the following, adapted from Arrowsmith (1988), as a starting-point.

Type of error	Treated by the teacher	Not treated
Content Grammatical Phonological Discourse Lexical Total treated Total not treated		

The ways that teacher responses to learner errors have been classified are particularly useful to the evaluator in the construction of observation schedules and checklists. The example of Chaudron (1977) below has examples from a French language learning class.

Feature or type of 'Act' (F and/or T)	Description	Example of exponent of expression
IGNORE (F)	Teacher (T) ignores Student's (S) ERROR, goes on to other topic, or shows ACCEPTANCE* of content.	
INTERRUPT (F)	T interrupts S utterance (ut) following ERROR, or before S has completed.	
DELAY (F)	T waits for S to complete ut. before correcting. (Usually not coded, for INTERRUPT is 'marked')	
ACCEPTANCE (T)	Simple approving or accepting word (usually as sign of reception of ut.), but T may immediately correct a linguistic ERROR.	Bon, oui, bien, d'accord
ATTENTION (T–F)	Attention-getter; probably quickly learned by Ss.	Euhh, regarde, attention, allez, maìs.
NEGATION (T–F)	T shows rejection of part or all of S ut.	Non, ne . . . pas.
PROVIDE (T)	T provides the correct answer when S has been unable or when no response is offered.	S: Cinquante, uh . . . T: Pour cent.
REDUCTION (F) (RED.)	T ut. employs only a segment of S ut.	S: Vee, eee . . . (spelling) T: Vé . .
EXPANSION (F) (EXP.)	T adds more linguistic material to S ut., possibly making more complete.	S: Et c'est bien. T: Ils ont pensé que c'était bien?
EMPHASIS (F) (EMPH.)	T uses stress, iterative repetition, or question intonation, to mark area or fact of incorrectness.	S: Mille. T: Mille?
REPETITION with NO CHANGE (T) (optional EXP. & RED.)	T repeats S ut. with no change of ERROR, or omission of ERROR	T: (les auto-routes) n'a pas de feux de circulation.
REPETITION with NO CHANGE and EMPH. (T) (F) (optional EXP. & RED.)	T repeats S ut. with no change of ERROR, but EMPH. locates or indicates fact of ERROR.	S: Mille. T: Mille?
REPETITION with CHANGE (T) (optional EXP. & RED.)	Usually T simply adds correction and continues to other topics. Normally only when EMPH. is added will correcting CHANGE become clear, or will T attempt to	S: Le maison est jaune. T: La maison est jaune.

(Chaudron 1977)

A large number of observational instruments have been developed over the years, for example Dunkin and Biddle (1974), Sinclair and Coulthard (1975), Mitchell, Parkinson, and Johnstone (1981). As Allen et al. (1983:232) point out:

'Observation schemes may differ with respect to a great variety of features, including type and number of content categories, coding procedures, units of analysis and source of the variables, as well as the purposes for which the instruments have been designed.'

Those interested in the analysis of classroom interaction and a review of different observational schedules used in this area are recommended to see Malamah-Thomas 1987, *Classroom Interaction*, in this Scheme.

Other procedures

The use of both video and audio recordings of classroom events can assist the data collection process. It is particularly valuable to review the recorded teaching and learning events and seek further explanations from the data. Field notes recorded by observers are useful additional sources of data. Another approach is a case study that focuses in depth on a particular issue, learner, or teacher. Further, secondary sources may contribute information for an evaluation. These appear in many forms including published articles or reports, school records, examiners' reports, and minutes from meetings. You may also wish to interview colleagues or learners. However, as Hopkins (1985:66) observes, interviews may be very time consuming and suggests 'it may be more profitable to devote time to general classroom meetings . . .'.

► TASK 51

Look again at the Scherer and Wertheimer evaluation examined in 3.2.

With reference to the procedures for gathering evaluative data described above, suggest ways in which this summative evaluation study of classroom methods could have been improved to provide descriptive data of use to a formative evaluation study.

Instead of emphasizing the outcomes of learning through the testing of learners, a closer examination of the different criterial features associated with the different hypothesized classroom methods should have been included. Such features incorporate the range of materials actually used in the classroom, the different methods employed by the teachers, the nature of interaction displayed by the learners under observation, the different learning tasks, and use of the first language and target language and the conditions in which each were used under the different instructional methods. You could also be more explicit in identifying your evaluation focal points:

- how teachers correct errors
- how learners respond to error correction
- how certain tasks promote collaborative work
- how learners carry out the same task in different ways
- how difficult some learners find certain types of test/test items
- how certain classroom materials work better than others
- how learners are better motivated in some classes than in others.

Additionally, the evaluation could have allowed for a regular evaluation of the programmes. Instead of waiting until the end of a long period of time (in the Scherer and Wertheimer study this was reported as two years), evaluation activities at more frequent intervals could have been introduced. In this way, a more comprehensive examination of the methods employed, and their regularity of use, would have been obtained.

The results of this study remain inconclusive. However, had classroom data been gathered at different time intervals across a range of predetermined criteria, the evaluators would have at least been able to make more precise statements about the different methodologies and materials used and learners' response to them. In other words, they would have been able to capture more accurately the real similarities and differences across methods in terms of actual classroom practice. The distinction between what is 'supposed to happen' in the classroom and 'what actually happens' in the classroom is crucial and is a point we emphasize throughout this book.

The data collection process
The process of collecting descriptive data for your evaluations is summarized as follows:

1 Select your setting, for example primary or secondary school context, tertiary ESP programme, EFL or language across the curriculum setting.
2 Identify what it is you wish to evaluate. Aim to narrow the focus of your evaluation as much as possible (so that you will not be 'taking too much on board').
3 Select or design your data collection procedures.
4 Collect the data
5 Describe the data collected.
6 Analyse these findings with reference to your initial purpose(s) for the evaluation, as specified in (2) above.

Summary
In the measurement-based approach to evaluation described above, the evaluator had a particular theory or hypothesis to test. But this does not have to be the case. In fact, there may be certain issues about which you, as evaluator, are not clear. Through your investigations you should be able to understand or explain the classroom phenomena in question more fully. Further, in the measurement-based tradition, tests are the main procedure for collecting data. However, descriptive data-based approaches select from a range of data collection instruments. Finally, measurement-based evaluations tend to be summative and focus on learning outcomes. These contrast with formative evaluations which yield information relating to the process of teaching and learning. Qualitative evaluation studies should therefore have a greater immediacy for language teaching specialists seeking to understand and evaluate classroom practices better. In **3.4** we focus on the role of the teacher in the evaluation process.

3.4 Evaluation and the classroom teacher

Role of teacher and external evaluator

'Ultimately, it is the teacher who has to operationalize on innovation at the classroom level.'
(Hoyle 1972:24, quoted in Stenhouse 1988:144)

Evaluation has frequently been conducted by 'experts'. In many cases they are not to any great extent part of the context in which the evaluation is taking place and, at worst, may have had no contact whatsoever. Although there are advantages to having different perspectives in an evaluation exercise (see **1.3**), these different contributions should maintain a certain balance of interests, both partial and impartial. If the development and planning of an evaluation becomes the responsibility of an external agent, such a balance cannot be achieved.

At one time it was widely held that evaluation could only be conducted by outsiders because this was the only way in which objectivity could be achieved. Objectivity at that time was considered a crucial criterion for the conduct of evaluations. It was felt that an insider such as a classroom teacher or an inspector was unsuitable because their judgements would be too subjective, i.e. that they would be unable to distance themselves from the object of the evaluation; this would be a 'bad' thing. There was concern about the possibility of biased data.

▶ **TASK 52**

What advantages do you see in involving the ELT practitioner, such as the teacher or an inspector, in evaluation activities?

It is important for users of an innovation to be involved in its evaluation. Firstly, the ELT practitioners know their context well, in many cases better than an external evaluator. The expert may know what questions to ask and how to obtain the relevant information, but teachers with experience gained over long periods of time have the advantage of being better able to explain and offer different and relevant interpretations of various classroom phenomena. Secondly, it is more likely that a classroom innovation or modification will be successfully implemented if the users of the innovation have contributed to its development. Thus, there is a place, as we have seen with the social interaction approach to innovation (see **1.3**), for all concerned parties to contribute to the development and evaluation process.

The tendency to rely on outsiders to do the evaluating has contributed to a certain reluctance on the part of teachers to analyse their curricular practices. This reluctance also arises from a feeling of inadequacy and lack of familiarity with the procedures for evaluating classrooms. However, it is the teachers who are experts on their own situations with major contributions to make to the evaluation of their own teaching and learning contexts.

It was Stenhouse (1975:143) who emphasized the unique role that teachers could play in the curriculum renewal process:

'... the uniqueness of each classroom setting implies that any proposal—even at school level—needs to be tested and verified and adapted by each teacher in his own classroom.'

Thus an approach to evaluation has developed in which the teacher is the initiator and the manager. This is what we look at next.

What kind of evaluation should teachers carry out?

The information for evaluating aspects of teaching and learning will be collected from the classroom itself using a variety of procedures selected from those described above (see **3.3**). For example, you might be interested in the amounts of time that you as a teacher spend talking to learners and what portion of your lesson time is available for the learners to speak. This would involve you in the analysis of classroom interaction (see Malamah-Thomas 1987).

Alternatively, you might want to evaluate the level of difficulty of a reading passage and its questions by means of a learner diary. You could ask some of your learners to write down some of the difficulties and reactions to a particular reading activity. The approach to classroom evaluation that will prove the most illuminating will be formative, focus on the process of teaching and learning, and be descriptive.

What can teachers evaluate in the classroom?

It is impossible to provide an exhaustive list of the issues and problems you may have identified, but some examples are given below.

1 To what extent are the materials I use suitable for the class?

2 As a teacher, to what extent do I use a learner-centred approach in my work?

3 Do the activities I give my learners to improve their fluency in language use actually achieve this aim?

4 In which ways are the traditional grammar exercises in the textbook inadequate?

5 Are the tests I have made for classroom use any more communicative than the ones I usually use?

6 How can I make my classes more interesting for my learners? They seem bored for much of the time.

7 With such large classes, how can I increase the amount of learner 'talk'?

8 How can I motivate my learners to use English outside the classroom?

▶ **TASK 53**

Take the question 'To what extent are the materials I use suitable for my class?' and make a list of some of the points you would consider in trying to answer this question.

Now check your points against those given below.

Question: 'To what extent are the materials suitable for use with this class?'

Answer: To address this question, I would need to take the following criteria into account:

1 Difficulty level, for example instructions or texts.
2 Length, for example of the reading and listening inputs. Are they too short, too long, or all right?
3 Instructions: are they clear and unambiguous?
4 Are the materials at the right level in terms of:
   a) linguistic level?
   b) conceptual level?
5 Student reaction: negative, positive, or indifferent?
6 Is there sufficient variety?
7 Is there a suitable range of materials?
8 Are they authentic? Is this important?
9 Is the format and layout clear?
10 Question types: is there a balance across open and closed question types?
11 Enjoyment and motivation.

▶ TASK 54

Consider the task of teaching. What aspects of your teaching might you wish to analyse further?

In this area, again, there is a wide range of issues to explore. You may have included some of the following in your list:

1 How much time do I spend talking in the classroom?
2 How do I correct errors?
3 How much feedback do I give my learners?
4 And how do I provide this feedback?
5 How much time do I allow for my learners to interact with each other?
6 How much of my lessons do I generally spend in teacher-fronted activities?
7 How can I improve my classroom management skills?
8 How much attention do I actually give to individual learners?

One of the main aims of self-analysis of a teacher's situation is to develop an awareness of what actually takes place in the classroom, when, and under what conditions. Evaluations of this type are not only concerned with aspects of classroom innovation but are also designed to raise the awareness of the teacher through the illumination of classroom practices. This, then, introduces a different purpose to the evaluation from judgements made when seeking out the inadequacies of a situation (see **2.2**).

How can teachers explore the classroom?
In **3.2** and **3.3** we examined various procedures that can be used in evaluations. But there is an additional approach that is particularly useful for the classroom teacher. This is known as *action research*, a term used for enquiries which aim to address specific issues of classroom practice on a small, local scale. It is evaluation undertaken by teachers and other ELT professionals for themselves in their own particular settings. Within this paradigm evaluation is seen as an important awareness-raising activity, and it has the advantage that issues and problems are identified and articulated locally, that is in the situation in which they naturally occur. Importantly, they are explored, described, and explained locally. As Jarvis (quoted in Brumfit 1984) states, the research:

'... is motivated by a specific local problem and is designed only to resolve that problem in that setting.'

The notion of action research is not a new concept; it was introduced by Kurt Lewin in the 1940s. His ideas have subsequently been modified and refined by educationists such as Stenhouse (1975), and others such as Parlett and Hamilton (1977), Kemmis and McTaggart (1982), McNiff (1988) and Whitehead (cited in McNiff, 1988). The procedure of action research is cyclic in nature and, in the words of Kemmis and McTaggart:

'To *do* action research one undertakes:
— to develop a *plan* of action to improve what is already happening,
— to *act* to implement the plan,
— to *observe* the effects of action in the context in which it occurs, and
— to *reflect* on these effects as a basis for further planning, subsequent action and so on, through a succession of cycles.'
(Kemmis and McTaggart 1982:7)

But, as Kemmis and McTaggart then observe, 'isn't this what every practitioner does?' This takes us back to points raised in **1.2** about the nature of evaluation and the importance of it being systematic and undertaken on a principled basis. Although practitioners do 'plan', 'act', 'observe', and 'reflect', this may not be done in any systematic and principled way. An example related to the evaluation of materials is presented next.

The issue
The textbook I use is structurally based. The writing exercises involve mainly the manipulation of structure and do not allow the learners the opportunity for freer practice in writing. The writing tests are also very

controlled. I would like to try to adapt some of these exercises to make them more communicative.

Planning

I draw up a list of features which I consider important to the communicative teaching and testing of writing. These include:

1 providing a realistic context for the writing task
2 providing a realistic purpose for writing
3 allowing learners freedom to use their own language
4 devising a task that focuses on meaning rather than form.

Acting

I devise a writing activity that incorporates the above features and give it in class. Afterwards, I ask some of the learners if they enjoyed this new type of activity.

Observing

I observe the learners doing the activity and make notes on (1) the questions the learners ask me and (2) learner reaction to the new task (using my general observations and my questions to individual learners).

Reflecting

The activity goes well in some respects but not in others. I noticed the learners showed more interest in the task than they usually do. But, since some of them didn't seem to know what they were supposed to do and appeared confused by the layout of the task, I need to simplify the explanation which relates to the context and audience of the task, and also to make my instructions more clear. Further, I realize I should have taken the class through this activity as a whole group first before getting them to work individually.

Planning

I decide to set up another similar task and to introduce it step by step with the whole class, allowing learners to ask questions as we go along. As we go through it, I shall emphasize points such as (1) the purpose of the task, (2) who they are writing to, and (3) what they are expected to do to complete the task successfully.

Acting

I introduce the next task as I had planned, taking the learners through the task before they get down to their own writing.

Observing

They were very interested in the context of the task and responded well to questions. They also initiated questions about the task. They all seemed quite happy in doing the writing.

Reflecting

These are some of the issues I need to think about more (and subsequently to 'act' on):

1 I realise I have said nothing to the learners about how I am going to assess their work. I should have let them know which criteria I am going to use.

2 I am wondering about the level of difficulty of this type of task for some of the weaker learners. Was it, for example, only two-thirds of the class who participated in the discussion? I can't remember how the weakest class members reacted.

3 Is it too soon to think about adapting some of the reading comprehension exercises in the textbook along similar lines?

4 Should I let my colleagues know about what I have been doing?

All these questions represent other aspects of my initial inquiry.

▶ **TASK 55**

Consider your own teaching and learning situation.

1 Identify an area of your work that you have tried to improve.

2 In terms of the categories planning, acting, observing, and reflecting, analyse what you planned and did, and what happened.

In her book, McNiff (1988) has reservations about the approach to action research adopted by Kemmis and McTaggart. She is of the view that their model is insufficiently flexible and responsive to the classroom context and proposes the following:

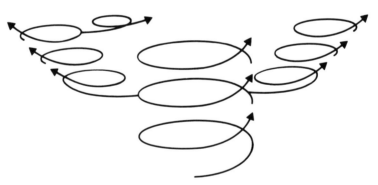

Figure 6 *A modified model of action research (McNiff 1988:45)*

As shown in Figure 6, and the above example related to the evaluation of materials, an evaluation of a specific issue will invariably raise a number of other and different issues. These could be wide ranging. In the same way as innovation brings both solutions to existing problems and new problems, so classroom evaluations will raise issues other than that being investigated initially.

3.5 Summary

In this section we have examined two approaches to carrying out evaluation.

1 A measurement-based approach emphasizes the testing of hypothesis using procedures such as tests; the results can be statistically analysed. The focus of such evaluations is product oriented and largely summative in nature, focusing on ends rather than means.

2 A descriptive data-based approach is concerned mainly with the gathering of new information with a view to forming new insights into aspects of language teaching and learning. Results expressed solely in quantitative terms have limited value in this type of enquiry, whereas information that is qualitatively expressed, in the form of descriptive or explanatory statements, is potentially much more informative. This is necessary since the primary concern is to capture and understand the reality of what happens in the classroom in order to retain what works and make appropriate changes.

We have also seen the important role that teachers and other ELT practitioners can and should play in the evaluation process, especially when evaluating aspects of classroom practice. Small-scale inquiries conducted along the lines of action research within practitioners' own contexts serve to clarify crucial pedagogic issues. More generally, they can contribute to a more efficient and effective working curriculum. The role of the external expert is more limited in this respect, whilst the contributions of the teacher assume far greater importance. The action research cycle presented here reflects a systematic approach to evaluation through which the principles of effective classroom practice may be described, explained, and evaluated.

4 A framework for curriculum evaluation

4.1 Introduction

In the preceding units we have examined the different purposes and principles behind curriculum evaluation. Here is a summary of the points raised in the form of a framework for evaluation activities consisting of eleven questions:

4.2 The evaluation framework

1 a) *Who* is the information for?
   b) *Why* are we carrying out the evaluation?
2 *What* will be evaluated? What aspect of the teaching and learning curriculum will be evaluated?
3 What are the *criteria* to be used in the evaluation? Who establishes these criteria?
4 *When* shall the evaluation take place? What are the time scales for the evaluation?
5 What *procedures* will be used to obtain the data?
6 Who/where are we going to get the information *from*?
7 Who are we going to *involve* in the evaluation?
8 *How* are we going to manage the evaluation?
9 What are we going to *do* with the information we get? This depends on:
   a) the purpose for the evaluation
   b) the nature of the evaluation
   c) the audience (to whom will the information be available?)
   d) the nature of the feedback from the evaluation
   e) the way in which the evaluation data is reported
10 What are the *constraints* and problems that need to be taken into account when planning for and implementing the evaluations?
11 *Evaluating* the evaluation process: are the evaluations effective?

▶   TASK 56

Think of an evaluation you would like to start. Consider each of the questions above and formulate your evaluation. Where necessary, refer back to relevant units in Section 1.

It is important to recognize the interdependence between these questions; the information elicited by the framework cannot be seen in isolation. For example, if you identify a need for evaluation for purposes of teacher development (question 1), this determines a range of other considerations: what will be evaluated (question 2), what evaluation criteria will be used (question 3), who you will involve in the evaluation (question 7), what you will do with the information obtained (question 9), and so on.

In question 10 we refer to constraints which need to be taken into account when planning and undertaking an evaluation. Some of these constraints we would expect to arise from the context in which the evaluation is taking place (see **1.5**). It is crucial to identify any constraints at the outset and to be aware of the effect(s) that these may have for the evaluation. You will also notice that in question 11 the new idea of keeping a track on the evaluations themselves was introduced. In other words, we feel it is important to evaluate the usefulness of any evaluations carried out. Are they achieving the purposes set? If they are not, is something being done about it?

4.3 Summary

The framework presented above is intended as a checklist and should be useful when preparing for evaluations. Each question raises some of the principles behind aspects of curriculum evaluation that have been examined in Section One. In Section Two, we shall see how these principles have been applied, and in Section Three you will be invited to apply these principles with reference to your own teaching and learning context.

Demonstration
The practice of evaluation

5   Project evaluation

5.1 Introduction

In Section One we defined and outlined the principles of evaluation. These were summarized in the form of an evalution framework presented in 4 above. In Section Two we now describe examples used to illustrate ways in which the evaluation of different aspects of the teaching and learning process have been carried out. We invite you to analyse these examples critically with reference to principles discussed earlier.

5.2 The Communicational Teaching Project (Bangalore)

The first example of evaluation is centred on the Communicational Teaching Project (henceforth CTP) initiated by N. S. Prabhu in Bangalore, South India. It has been chosen for several reasons. Not only has it attracted a considerable amount of professional interest over the past few years but it is well documented. It also represents an innovation in foreign language learning in a non-privileged and non-idealized situation with large classes as the norm, few resources, and a minimum of technology.

5.3 The context

The CTP was set up in 1979 in selected primary schools. It emerged as a response to a general disillusionment with the ways in which structure was taught in schools. The CTP syllabus addresses the issue of *how* learners may most effectively learn grammar. It differs from the typically graded structural oral situational syllabus in that it is made up of a series of tasks in the form of problem-solving (rather than structure-focused) activities relating to, for example, school timetables, maps, programmes, and itineraries (Prabhu 1987:139). These learning activities aim to focus on 'meaning or thinking which such problem solving necessarily brings about' (Prabhu 1982). Since one of the main hypotheses of the CTP is that language form is best learnt when the learner's attention is focused on meaning, this project may be seen less as an attempt to change syllabus content and rather more as an innovation in the area of classroom methodology.

5.4 Aims

An evaluation was undertaken by Beretta and Davies (1985) after learners had been in the CTP for several years. The evaluation aims have been described as follows:

'to assess through appropriate tests, whether there is any demonstrable difference in terms of attainment in English between classes of children who have been taught on the CTP and their peers who have received normal instruction in the respective schools.'
(Beretta and Davies 1985:121–2)

▶ TASK 57

In Section One (see **2.2**) a distinction was made between summative evaluation (i.e. that takes place after a period of time) and formative evaluation (i.e. that has awareness-raising goals, that focuses on the process of teaching and learning, and provides information that can be used for developmental purposes).

From the aims of the CTP evaluation described above:
How would you describe the main focus of the evaluation?
Is there an emphasis on:
a) summative evaluation?
b) formative evaluation?

5.5 Design and procedures

The approach adopted for this evaluation was a traditional experimental design approach. Six schools were involved altogether. Those in the regular classes (the control groups) used the usual teaching materials organized along formal structural lines. The CTP classes (the experimental groups) used problem-solving activities, for example, interpretation of a map or a timetable. The principal differences, therefore, between the classes taught within the CTP and those receiving normal (structural) instruction lie in the learning materials and the methodology. A battery of tests was constructed to measure learning outcomes separately for experimental and control groups by a structure test and a CTP task-based test. Achievement tests were designed as measures of each method, while proficiency tests were intended to be neutral of method and required some degree of transfer from classroom practice (Beretta and Davies 1985:123).

5.6 Findings

The results of this evaluation revealed that the experimental and control groups did significantly better on their own achievement tests. There was also some evidence to suggest that the CTP groups performed better on the proficiency tests.

▶ TASK 58

Examine the evaluation design, procedures, and results presented above.

1 How would you describe the main purpose for the evaluation:
   a) accountability?
   b) curriculum development?
   c) teacher development?

2 How could the results obtained be used, and by whom?

The evaluation was undertaken in 1984, thus examining the CTP several years after it was set up (1979). Its focus is clearly on the outcomes of the teaching and learning project expressed in terms of learner products. The aim of the evaluation is therefore summative.

The CTP was intended to bring about changes in methodology; the teaching to be concerned with creating conditions for coping with meaning in the classroom as opposed to the manipulation of grammatical forms. In other words, issues of methodology were of key importance for this project.

▶ TASK 59

1 What aspects of methodology do you think were actually evaluated?

2 Would you feel happy that the methodology was comprehensively evaluated using tests as the sole evaluation procedure?

There are clearly limitations in terms of the way that the overall value of the CTP was formally evaluated, largely because a principled evaluation was not set up at the outset. In fact, no evaluative data was provided that would suggest areas in which curriculum improvements could be made. It would therefore have been desirable for an alternative, pedagogically motivated evaluation to have been formally integrated within the CTP; one that was formative in focus and capable of describing and analysing the strengths and weaknesses of the teaching and learning process.

▶   TASK 60

1 If you wanted to compare two different methods of teaching, what are the kinds of things you would be looking for?

2 The CTP involved two types of methodology, structural and communicational. What do you think could have been evaluated in this project?

A comprehensive formative evaluation of the CTP, in contrast with the summative evaluation conducted by Beretta and Davies, would have looked at a greater range of classroom events and processes. Greenwood (1985) specifically drew attention to the need 'for more appropriate and illustrative evidence of the materials and methodology' used in the CTP. In the Beretta and Davies (1985) study we have no information about how learners participated in the two types of class. Nor do we know whether the teaching method was really different in the CTP classes.

When we are looking at what makes for effective learning (effective teaching) then formative evaluation is the key. By the time you carry out a summative evaluation it is too late! In many ways, the process of teaching and learning has already stopped.

5.7 Summary

Many curriculum evaluations have focused on product evaluations, by measuring the extent to which learners have mastered the programme content. Evaluation of the process of learning in the curriculum should not be overshadowed. Both can be done. This is demonstrated in some of the evaluation activities that follow.

6 Evaluation of methodology

6.1 Introduction

One of the important aspects of the CTP discussed above was methodology and this is a central question addressed in the work of Spada (1987) who evaluated the nature of 'communicative' language teaching. For this, she used a specially designed observational schedule (Fröhlich, Spada, and Allen 1985).

6.2 The context

The classrooms investigated by Spada involved adult learners enrolled in three classes of an intensive ESL programme at an English-speaking university in Canada.

6.3 Aims

The study investigated:

1 whether there were differences in the kind of instruction that learners in a communicative programme were receiving;
2 whether differences in instruction contributed to variation in learners' improvement and proficiency.

Whereas Beretta and Davies (1985) focused attention almost exclusively on learning outcomes, Spada examined not only learning outcomes but also instructional processes.

6.4 Design and procedures

Data were collected in two ways. Firstly, in order to determine the learners' level of language proficiency, a pre-test was administered at the beginning of the course and a post-test at the end of the programme. Secondly, the COLT (communicative orientation of language teaching) observation scheme was used in an attempt to discriminate between different types of classroom and to identify those factors which may be contributing to learning. Classes were observed for five hours a day, once a week for four out of the six weeks of the study. This provided twenty hours of observation data per class.

▶ TASK 61

There are many features you can associate with a communicative classroom. If you were to devise an observation checklist to analyse the features of your classroom, what categories would you wish to include, for example, classroom interaction: teacher to learner, learner to teacher, learner(s) to learner(s)?

As we saw in **3.3** (on pages 62 and 63), the COLT observation scheme is divided into two parts.

Part A (Spada 1987:142) describes what happens in the classroom in terms of the different activities under five major categories:

1 *Activities*: the kinds of exercises and tasks learners are required to do in the classroom;

2 *Participant organization*: how much time is spent on different kinds of interaction, for example, learner-learner versus teacher-learner interaction;

3 *Content*: the extent to which the teaching focuses on meaning or on form (language code); the 'language' category focuses on code-related teaching whereas 'other topics' relates to the range of reference of topics (broad to narrow) within teaching that is meaning-focused; 'topic control' relates to who (teacher or learner) controls the topics dealt with in class;

4 *Student modality* describes how much time learners spend practising the four language skills;

5 *Materials*: type, length, source of learning materials used.

Part B of the COLT observation scheme focuses on the communicative features of verbal exchange between teachers and learners or learners themselves as they occur within each activity:

TEACHER VERBAL INTERACTION

TARGET LANG.		INFORMATION GAP				SUST. SPEECH		REACTION CODE/MES.	INCORPORATION of S. UTTERANCES					
		Giving Info.		Request Info.										
L1	L2	Predict	Unpred.	Pseudo	Genuine	Minimal	Sustained	Explicit Code Reaction	No Incorp.	Repetition	Paraphrase	Comment	Expansion	Elaboration

STUDENT VERBAL INTERACTION

TARGET LANG.		Disc. Initiation	INFORMATION GAP				SUST. SPEECH			FORM RESTR.			REACTION CODE/MES.	INCORPORATION of S/T UTTERANCES					
			Giving Info.		Request Info.														
L1	L2		Pred.	Unpred.	Pseudo	Genuine	Ultraminimal	Minimal	Sustained	Restricted	Limited	Unrestricted	Explicit Code Reaction	No Incorp.	Repetition	Paraphrase	Comment	Expansion	Elaboration

(Fröhlich, Spada, and Allen 1985:57)

▶ TASK 62

From the information given in **6.3** and **6.4**, how is the evaluation best described?

1 Identify where the focus is on:
   a) classroom processes
   b) learning outcomes

2 In what way does Spada evaluate learning outcomes summatively?

3 To what extent is there a formative focus on the analysis of the teaching process?

6.5 Findings

Here we focus on some of Spada's findings. The first set of findings presented are expressed quantitatively in the form of tables. Two examples follow:

*Student Modality: Total percentage of time spent on one modality by class**

Feature	Class A	Class B	Class C
Listening	55.36	45.55	39.81
Speaking	22.82	24.66	25.04
Reading	15.40	22.12	19.65
Writing	6.16	6.15	14.91

* For a breakdown of the percentage of time spent on a primary and combined skills focus, see Table 13 in the Appendix.

*Materials—Text, Mode, Source: Total percentage of time spent on a primary focus on minimal/extended, audio/visual and pedagogic/non-pedagogic materials by class**

Feature		Class A	Class B	Class C
Text:	Minimal	39.97	16.25	16.30
	Extended	22.96	55.74	41.37
Mode:	Audio	10.00	14.07	10.30
	Visual	1.77	0.09	0.0
Source:	Pedagogic	48.30	48.02	14.20
	Non-pedagogic	26.72	13.38	25.32

* These percentages do not add up to 100 because materials were not used at all times.

Table 4 *(Spada 1987:146–7)*

▶ TASK 63

Analyse the results presented above with reference to the question: Were there differences in the kinds of instruction that learners in a communicative programme were receiving?

Further findings are given below:

'Another difference which emerged from the qualitative analysis was the way in which certain activities were carried out, particularly with respect to listening activities. For example, in classes B and C the instructors tended to start each listening activity with a set of predictive exercises. Presumably, these were intended to generate learners' interest in the subject matter and to help them anticipate the contents of the listening passage. This was usually followed by a reading of the comprehension questions by the teacher to prepare learners for the precise information they were expected to listen to. The next step most often involved playing a section of a tape-recorder passage and stopping when necessary to allow requests for clarification and repetition. Also, instructors in both classes tended to focus explicitly on the kinds of strategies they were teaching, so that learners were made aware of the fact that a particular exercise was intended to improve their abilities in listening for specific information, whereas another was for developing global or overall comprehension skills. In class A, however, the listening activities were dealt with somewhat differently. Learners were given a list of comprehension questions to read silently to themselves, and they were free to ask the teacher for assistance if they did not understand any of the questions. An audio-recorded passage was then played in its entirety, usually twice, while the learners answered comprehension questions.'
(Spada 1987:144–5)

▶ TASK 64

Study the qualitative results that Spada reports above.

1 What do you consider to be the most important findings from these classroom observations?

2 What inferences can you draw from the findings about class A and classes B and C?

3 Which set of data—quantitative (see the examples of Spada's tables above) or qualitative (see the extract from Spada's report above)—provides the most information?

4 Could the information derived from the observation of classes been obtained in any other ways?

Although there are other ways in which information may be gained about what goes on in classrooms, for example, teacher self-reports, learner diaries, or interviews, observation is an important tool in capturing the reality of classrooms. This is fully recognized in Spada's work.

▶ ## TASK 65

With reference to the evaluation of the Communicational Teaching Project described in 5 above, what do you perceive as the main differences between the two approaches (the CTP and Spada) to evaluation?

6.6 Summary

Spada approached the evaluation of classrooms from both a quantitative (numbers) and qualitative (description and explanation) point of view. It represents an example of an evaluation undertaken by an external 'expert'. However, in the way that she has approached this work, Spada has demonstrated the importance of observation in understanding better what actually happens in classrooms. In Section Three, we shall provide opportunities for evaluations in which observation has an important role to play.

7 Evaluation of a foreign language teaching programme

7.1 Introduction

Here we look at an evaluation of foreign language teaching in a secondary school context, sometimes referred to as the Stirling evaluation. Like the work of Spada, systematic classroom observation is a major focus of this work. In this evaluation, a variety of different aspects of classroom practice are investigated. Only a sample of these are discussed here.

7.2 The context and aims

This evaluation was conducted during the school year 1977–8 and aims to 'provide a systematic description of classroom practice in eight schools, involving the use of a conventional audio-visual foreign language course' (Mitchell, Parkinson, Johnstone 1981:1). It concentrates on the foreign language teaching process, in this case the teaching of French as a foreign language. The evaluation reported here was undertaken in first year secondary schools in Stirling, Scotland, in order to find out what were the actual classroom practices. As the evaluators indicate in their introduction (1981:2), 'this study provides an account of the extent to which a particular group of teachers displayed or failed to display a range of 'desirable' behaviours.'

▶ TASK 66

1 Given the above brief for the evaluation, how would you best describe the main purpose for the evaluation:
a) accountability?
b) curriculum development?
c) teacher development?

2 In what ways can an evaluation of this kind be useful to classroom teachers?

The intentions of those who carried out the evaluation were (1) to produce a descriptive account of current practice in foreign language teaching in classroom settings, and (2) to evaluate current teaching practices in relation to the most recent principles (i.e. at that time) of modern language teaching, with a view of bringing about improvements in methodology. Thus the evaluation was undertaken for curriculum development purposes, which also entails teacher self-development.

▶ TASK 67

What sort of evaluation instruments (procedures) would you use in such an evaluation? For example, if you were to observe classes, would you use a checklist? If so, what form might it take?

7.3 Design and procedures

Introduction
Systematic observation was one of the three main procedures used to evaluate the foreign language classrooms. The other two used were tests and interviews. These evaluation techniques are described below.

Observation
An observation scheme was used to analyse the language lessons systematically. These were divided up into segments, ten minute units, which were observed using the following five main categories:

1 *The topic of discourse*: what was being talked about in the lessons.
2 *Language activity*: the range of language activities planned and directed by the teacher.
3 *Teacher mode of involvement*: the relationship of the teacher to the pupils in any segment: their role in the discourse.
4 *Pupil mode of involvement*: how the teachers expected pupils to involve themselves with the teaching segments.
5 *Class organization*: the patterns of classroom organization planned and put into action by the teacher.

Below we look at two of these categories to give us an indication of the ways in which observation schedules can be organized.

Language activity
This refers to the range, i.e. variety and balance, of language activities used by a teacher. It also involves a consideration of the extent to which the foreign language is used for communicative purposes in the classroom. This dimension was examined under different headings as follows (Mitchell et al. 1981:17, adapted):

1 Translation: lexical meanings made explicit through the first language.

2 First language: all discourse in the mother tongue.

3 Real foreign language: where the foreign language is used for real messages and the focus is on meaning.

4 Transposition: practice in written and spoken modes with a focus on the relationship between them.

5 Presentation: practice in global comprehension in listening or reading activities.

6 Imitation: pupils imitate foreign language models, for example repetition or copy writing.

7, 8 Drill/exercise: focus is on syntactic form or appropriateness.

9 Compound: brief occurrences of more than one of the above.

Class organization
Within this category data is collected about the ways in which the teacher organizes the class. This dimension was analysed as follows (Mitchell et al. 1981:19):

1 Whole class: one central activity where the whole class functions as a group.

2 Pupil demonstration: one central activity demonstrated by one pupil.

3 Cooperative, same task: cooperative group work with identical tasks.

4 Cooperative, different tasks: cooperative group work with different tasks.

5 Individual, same task: pupils working alone, without cooperation, all on the same task.

6 Individual, different tasks: as (5) except that some individuals have different tasks.

7 Cooperative, individual: some working cooperatively but others individually. Tasks may be either the same or different.

▶ **TASK 68**

Select one of the dimensions above that would be useful for you to analyse your own classroom practice. Draw up a sample observation schedule for the dimension chosen.

Findings from the observation of classes
In relation to the category 'language activity', limitations in the syllabus were found. The breakdown of 'language activity' was given in the evaluation as a table of language activity frequencies.

Language activity	Mean segment length	Absolute frequency (no. segments)	Relative frequency (%)
Translation	2.6 min	176	10.6
First language	2.1	353	21.3
Foreign language	1.9	30	1.8
Transposition	2.6	123	7.4
Presentation	1.6	114	6.9
Imitation	2.7	203	12.3
Drill/exercise	4.3	573	34.6
Compound	5.9	84	5.1
Total	3.2	1656	100.0

Table 5 Class observation findings *(Mitchell et al. 1981:30)*

▶ TASK 69

Analyse the findings presented in the table above.

1 How much classroom time was spent on the use of the foreign language for communicative purposes?

2 How much time was spent on the manipulation of language form?

3 How would you describe the overall approach to teaching, as reflected in the findings of this table?

On close analysis, intensive repetition and manipulation of restricted sets of language forms is revealed in the table above, with a frequency of 12.3 per cent for imitation activities and 34.6 per cent for drills and exercises. Real use of the foreign language has a frequency of only 1.8%. There is thus a significant absence of the communicative use of the foreign language.

Oral testing

A part of this evaluation also focused on pupil outcomes. To gain insights into the communicative orientation of the course a ten minute oral test was administered to 94 pupils. The aim was twofold, (1) to get a general idea of the levels of achievement near the end of the first year, and (2) to explore some tentative relationships between the pupil performances and the teaching processes (an aim similar to that of Spada described in 6 above).

The test was an achievement test related to the content of the teaching syllabus, i.e. the first six units of the coursebook. It had fifty oral questions which were audio-recorded and later transcribed for scoring. Four types of item were tested (1981:48):

1 Questions about two sequences or pictures taken from early units of the coursebook.

2 Personal questions about pupils and their school day.

3 A simple oral composition, based on one of the sets of pictures already discussed through question and answer.

4 Brief phrases in English for translation into French.

▶ TASK 70

'The test retained a degree of flexibility, and in particular did not impose rigid structural control on the utterances produced by pupils' (1981:48).

This comment was made in the evaluation report. From the information you have been given:

1 Do you think that the test shows flexibility?

2 What part do you think that the test played in the overall evaluation? Does it, in your opinion, actually contribute to a better evaluation?

In scoring the test, four criteria were used:

1 Comprehension and minimum response: could the pupil understand without prompting?

2 Comprehension and communication: could the pupil understand and give an appropriate response in French?

3 Production of target structures: could the pupil produce a range of structures from the course units one to six?

4 Narration: could the pupil produce a connected narrative prompted by pictures, matched against criteria of (a) accuracy and (b) cohesion?

▶ TASK 71

To what extent do the scoring criteria given above differ from the types of criteria used in tests with which you are familiar?

Findings from the oral testing
The finding of the test can be summarized as follows. Overall, pupils showed an incomplete mastery of all the core structures and the other areas tested.

▶ TASK 72

From the limited information you have been given on pupil evaluation:

1 What do you think about the suitability of the test in terms of level? Was it too difficult or set at the correct level?

2 Do you think the results show the full extent of pupil attainment? What factors might have influenced the findings?

Interviews with teachers
A third way information was collected was through open-ended interviews with sixteen teachers. They were asked generally about their priorities in first year French teaching.

Findings from interviews with teachers
For fifteen out of the sixteen teachers, developing foreign language competence meant oral skills. One teacher held that writing was also a priority. Those who mentioned oral skills judged oral performance by the following criteria: fluency and structural accuracy (six teachers), correct pronunciation (five teachers), developing understanding (three teachers), and vocabulary building (three teachers). Other issues that emerged from the interviews included the development of positive attitudes towards the French language and foreign language learning (seven teachers) and the need to impart positive attitudes towards France and French culture as a regular feature of French lessons (five teachers).

▶ TASK 73

1 What do you see as the advantages and disadvantages of using interviews as an evaluation procedure?

2 It appears that the interview used in the Stirling evaluation was a relatively unstructured one. Compare this procedure with the one described in **14.4** (page 124). What do you perceive as the essential differences between the two types of interview?

7.4 Feedback from the evaluation

We have looked at only some of the information that resulted from the classroom evaluation. Below are some extracts of other findings from the Stirling evaluation (1981:66–7).

'From this process there has emerged a picture of these classrooms as busy, work-oriented places, with a heavy emphasis on oral FL activities. The teachers observed were in almost constant interaction with their classes, whose members were expected to attend to, and to produce, large quantities of spoken French . . .'

However, these large amounts of oral FL usage were limited in several ways. Most of the observed FL activities involved the intensive, repetitive manipulation of very restricted sets of language elements; extensive exposure to any richer FL diet was very rare. Additionally, . . . a 'content vacuum' was apparent in many lessons; if a coherent topic of discourse could be identified at all (and in many FL segments this was not the case), it appeared to have the primary function of a peg on which to hang imitative or manipulative practice in the coursebook language syllabus . . .

The pupils in the classes we studied received virtually identical language experiences, which moreover centred always on the teacher. Group and individual work were rare, and differentiation in the tasks set even rarer; even reading was overwhelmingly a whole-class, lock-step activity . . .'

There follows an interpretation of these findings with a view to formulating plans for future action.

▶   TASK 74

    1 What would be your interpretation of the evaluation findings presented above?
    2 What recommendations would you make on the basis of this data for future action, with a view to both teacher and curriculum development?

The findings from an evaluation have of course to be analysed within the context from which they have been drawn. Thus, in the case of the Stirling evaluation of an audiolingual programme, it could be said that the move at that time (i.e. mid- to late-seventies) had been reasonably successful in stressing the importance of the spoken word. On the other hand, given the comments on the lack of coherent 'content' of lessons and a real-life exchange of meanings, it could be said that there was an almost total absence of the communicative use of French. In terms of our current understanding of the importance of classroom interaction, of a rich and varied input, of giving pupils the opportunity to express their own meanings, one would now be concerned by the limited patterns of teaching in the classes observed. All these interpretations have implications for future innovations in these foreign language classrooms.

7.5 Summary

The Stirling evaluation of a French programme, with specific reference to the teaching approach in use, has shown us how different procedures may each produce important findings. Those used in this evaluation were classroom observation schedules, pupil tests, and questionnaires and interviews for teachers. Although this particular evalution was conducted by external evaluators, classroom teachers were involved in the overall evaluation process. However, there is no reason why teachers, individually, in pairs or in groups, could not begin an evaluation of their own classrooms using some of the ideas raised in both the Spada and Stirling evaluation studies.

The next evaluation example follows on from the work of both Spada and Mitchell et al.; it also uses observation as a means to examine classrooms. However, it takes as its focus one aspect of classroom practice and looks at how one teacher deals with errors.

8   Evaluating teacher feedback on oral errors

8.1 Introduction

As we saw in Section One, one of the main issues in evaluation is to inquire into the possible disparity between what teachers think they do and what they actually do. Here we report on an evaluation of error treatment undertaken by four MA students (Arrowsmith, Linghai, Jurado-Spruch, and Miletto 1988/89) at Ealing College (now Polytechnic of West London) as part of their MA Classroom Studies option. This work focused on the nature of classroom feedback provided to second language learners in the form of teacher treatment of oral errors and was partly motivated by the view that 'teachers in general do not appear to have a coherent policy, or even a high degree of awareness regarding their classroom practice on the subject of error treatment' (Arrowsmith 1988:5).

8.2 Aims

The aims of this study were to evaluate 'the relationship between an individual teacher's expressed attitude to the correction of oral errors, and his actual treatment of oral errors in the classroom' (Arrowsmith 1988:1). The focus was on different types of error and how they were dealt with in a class.

▶   TASK 75

    1 How could an evaluation of this kind be useful for purposes of:
      a) accountability?
      b) curriculum development?
      c) teacher self-development?

    2 In what specific ways do you think an evaluation of this kind would be useful to teachers?

The information obtained from such an evaluation could, of course, be used in a judgemental way for purposes of accountability. However, it is more likely to be of use to individual teachers than to heads of schools or similar organizations. As we saw earlier, our perceptions of ourselves as teachers do not always match the reality of what happens in practice. An evaluation like this has the potential, therefore, to provide invaluable formative feedback to teachers on the ways in which they actually deal with errors in the classroom context. As such, an evaluation of this kind functions as an important means to teachers' self-development.

8.3 Design and procedures

The evaluation involved an experienced teacher of an adult ESL beginners' class. The fourteen students enrolled in his class were from different language backgrounds.

▶ TASK 76

What procedures would you use to collect information about how a teacher deals with errors in the classroom?

In the study data were collected in three ways:

1 real-time observation using an observation schedule;
2 a video recording of the lesson;
3 a structured interview with the teacher (also videoed).

A number of other procedures such as a diary or checklist would also have been appropriate.

Observation schedule
Firstly, the categories included in the observation schedule were based largely on earlier work on error correction such as Allwright (1975) and Chaudron (1977). These included:

1 a) 'content' errors, i.e. not about the language itself but about the topic being discussed.
   b) 'formal' errors, i.e. phonological, grammatical, discourse, handwriting, and spelling.
2 how errors were dealt with, i.e. ignored or dealt with a) by the teacher or b) by another pupil.
3 teacher's manner of correction, for example immediate or delayed, repetition, rephrasing.

Structured interview
Secondly, the questions in the interview mirrored those points included on the observation schedule, as well as questions designed to get at the basic principles underlying the teacher's correction policy. This interview was recorded on video.

Structured questionnaire
Thirdly, a questionnaire was used to provide additional information. Here are some extracts.

This questionnaire is concerned with your policy regarding error correction with Class 1A.

Please circle the relevant number.

1 How frequently do you feel it desirable to correct errors made during classroom oral interaction, overall?

all the time				never
5	4	3	2	1

2 How desirable is it to correct the following errors with this class?

a) phonological

v. imp.				not at all imp.
5	4	3	2	1

b) lexical

v. imp.				not at all imp.
5	4	3	2	1

c) grammatical

v. imp.				not at all imp.
5	4	3	2	1

d) discourse, for example errors of style, organization and appropriacy

v. imp.				not at all imp.
5	4	3	2	1

e) content

v. imp.				not at all imp.
5	4	3	2	1

3 State how important you consider the following principles to be with regard to your error correction policy with this class.

It is desirable to correct errors that:

a) are relevant to the pedagogic focus of the activity/lesson.

v. imp.				not imp.
5	4	3	2	1

b) occur frequently during a lesson/activity whether or not they are part of the pedagogic focus of the lesson, i.e.:

1 during accuracy work

v. imp.				not imp.
5	4	3	2	1

2 during fluency work	v. imp.				not imp.
	5	4	3	2	1
c) are produced by a number of learners	v. imp.				not imp.
	5	4	3	2	1
d) affect communication	v. imp.				not imp.
	5	4	3	2	1

(Arrowsmith et al. 1988)

► TASK 77

Answer the questions on the questionnaire above to find out what you think you do when correcting errors in the classroom. (Keep your responses for comparison later in **17.1**, Task 107.)

The observation data were collected during a two-hour lesson. Only errors and feedback arising from teacher-whole-class interactions were noted. After this observation, the class teacher was given the questionnaire to complete followed by an interview three days later.

► TASK 78

1 If you were to do an evaluation like this, who else would you involve in the collection and analysis of data?
2 Suggest ways in which learners could be involved in analysing how errors are treated in class.

As an example, when teachers review their lesson on video, the learners could be invited to comment on what they thought the teacher was doing and what they themselves were doing when the focus was on the correction of errors. In evaluations it is important to collect views from a variety of relevant participants.

8.4 Findings

The results were reported under two main headings:

The teacher's expressed attitude to error treatment
The teacher's responses from the questionnaire and the interview revealed several attitudes towards correcting errors.

1 If the learning activity was 'communicative', errors were largely ignored. In form-focused activities, however, there would be greater attention to formal errors.

2 Errors relating to the teaching aim of the lesson would be attended to both during teacher-centred and small group work. However, incidental errors would only be treated at the pair/group work stage.

3 Error correction would depend on the type of learners. In the case of a weak learner, it might be demoralizing to pick up errors; for the stronger learner error correction could be motivating.
(*Arrowsmith 1988:10*)

The teacher's actual attitude to error treatment
An analysis of the evaluation data revealed a large amount of information regarding:

1 the overall occurrence of errors;
2 the proportion of errors dealt with;
3 the nature of feedback on error, for example, location of error or indicating the fact of an error;
4 the manner of correction;
5 the range of features in feedback techniques.

The evaluation also revealed a certain inconsistency in terms of what teachers thought they did and what they actually did. Interestingly, some of these inconsistencies can be explained by key variables that affect teacher behaviour within the learning activities themselves and also towards different learners. These related to relevance to the aims of the lesson, focus on accuracy or fluency (see part (b) of question 3 of the structured questionnaire above), time available, and the needs of individual learners.

8.5 Summary

This classroom evaluation addressed the following question: How closely does this teacher's expressed attitude to the treatment of oral errors mirror actual classroom practice? The importance of an evaluation of this kind lies in its value as an awareness-raising device by teacher trainers or by teachers themselves. It provides information that gives teachers an opportunity to develop their understanding of the factors involved in the giving of feedback on errors and the possible effects of any lack of clarity or ambiguity on their students.

We now turn to the evaluation of classroom learning materials.

9 Evaluation of materials: dictionaries

West (1987) presents an example of one of the ways in which book resources may be evaluated.

9.1 The context

During in-service workshops for teachers, West examined the 'ever-increasing range of dictionaries' that are commercially available for English language learners. The evaluation was restricted to monolingual dictionaries intended for non-native speakers of English.

9.2 Aims

The principal aim of the evaluation was to determine appropriate criteria for the evaluation of these dictionaries and then to use them to make comparisons across the range of dictionaries on the market. This would then help teachers and learners to choose the right dictionary for their purposes.

► TASK 79

Make a list of criteria that you think would be relevant for evaluating dictionaries available in your context.

9.3 Design and procedures

In the workshops the teachers discussed various evaluation criteria. West reports on ten of these:

1 UK price, format, and date
2 Number of pages
3 Level/coverage
4 Workbooks
5 Pronunciation
6 Ease of use
7 Definitions
8 Grammatical assistance
9 Illustrations
10 Appendices

Once the criteria were established, these were applied to four categories of dictionary (West 1987:59):

1 Dictionaries for the advanced learner
2 Dictionaries for learners at lower levels
3 Pocket dictionaries
4 ESP dictionaries

▶   TASK 80

Examine the evaluation criteria listed above. Consider the distinctions made in **2.4** and identify which ones are appropriate to the
evaluation of dictionaries:
a) at the level of workplan (aims);
b) at the level of use (implementation);
c) at the level of learner outcomes (product).

9.4 Findings

Below we illustrate the way in which the evaluation criteria were applied
to two dictionaries:

Title	Oxford–Duden Pictorial English Dictionary	Longman Active Study Dictionary	
Date & format	1981 h/b + p/b	1983 p/b	
Number of pages	824	710	
Level/ coverage	Intermediate + above+ ESP 28,000	Intermediate 38,000 entries	
Workbook available? Quality?	no	yes ■ ■ ■ ■	
Pronunciation	n/a	IPA	
Ease of use	■ ■ ■ ■ Thematically arranged; good index	■ ■ ■ ■	
Definitions	Pictures only	■ ■ ■ ■ Uses 2000-word vocab.	
Grammatical assistance	□	■ ■ ■	
Illustrations	■ ■ ■ ■	■ ■	**Key**
Number of appendices	—	3	h/b = hardback p/b = paperback n/a = not applicable
Comments	Extensive and clear. Superb illustrations, some in colour. Specialist coverage surpasses most ESP dictionaries.	Best buy in this category for combining good coverage and examples with built-in workbook and exercises.	□ = not recommended ■ ■ = fair ■ ■ ■ = recommended ■ ■ ■ ■ = good

(West 1987:70 and 73)

▶ TASK 81

> 1 Analyse the ratings given to the two dictionaries above. Which one would you buy on the basis of the information given above?
>
> 2 What other criteria do you think it would have been useful to include in an evaluation of this kind?

9.5 Summary

As with many evaluations concerning materials, the focus implicit in the work reported by West is evaluation at the workplan stage, i.e. considering the products on the bookshop shelf. However, we find it noteworthy that in his conclusion West chooses to comment on the fact that the evaluation workshops were very interesting from the point of view of how the teachers actually use dictionaries in the classroom. Here he is highlighting an evaluation criterion at the level of actual classroom use which is not reflected in most of the evaluation criteria used in his own study. (For further information, see **18** below.)

Book reviews are another way in which it is possible to evaluate books and learning materials. They can provide information to help you choose a particular textbook or to encourage you to look around for something more appropriate for your purposes. In the next section, we look at a review of a grammar book.

10 Evaluation of materials: book reviews

10.1 Introduction

Book reviews are included in most EFL newspapers and journals. They introduce readers to new material and help teachers to evaluate new books as they become available. However, we must guard against uncritically accepting the word of a book reviewer. What criteria do we have in judging a review? What information is given us by the reviewer so that we can make decisions about a textbook? Some criteria used to judge a book are defined below.

10.2 The context and aims

The following book review on 'An A–Z of English Grammar and Usage' appeared in the *EFL Gazette* (February 1990, No. 122:22). This monthly newspaper includes reviews of EFL books and materials.

▶ TASK 82

What sort of information would you find useful in a book review to help you decide to look further at a particular book? List some of the items.

At a first level, it might be useful to you to have some basic information about the author, publisher, and the cost of the book. Usually you will find that kind of information first. Then it is often a good idea to establish who the reviewer is and the reviewer's background. The published review begins:

An A-Z of English Grammar and Usage. Geoffrey Leech (associate authors – Benita Cruickshank and Roz Ivanic), *Edward Arnold, £5.25*

Felicity O'Dell

There is currently quite a variety of grammar books for the EFL student and teacher to choose from and Professor Leech has now turned from writing more academic grammar textbooks to add one rather simpler grammar to the range.

Information about the reviewer is also given, generally at the end of the review:

> *Felicity O'Dell is a Senior Teacher at Eurocentre, Cambridge, and the co-author (with Roy Kingsbury) of* **Using Grammar** *(Longman).*

▶ TASK 83

Information about the author and the reviewer appears in the above extract of the review, for example that Geoffrey Leech is an academic. What other information is given about the authors and the reviewer?

Moving on to the next part of the review, the format of the book is compared to that of another well-known grammar book (Michael Swan, *Practical English Usage*):

> The format of this book is reminiscent of Michael Swan's *Practical English Usage* in that it presents the different points discussed alphabetically beginning with 'a or an,' 'a-words' (*against, aboard, afraid* etc) and 'a bit of' and concluding with 'zero plural', 'zero relative pronoun' and 'zero that-clause'.

This comparison is explained further in the next paragraph of the review. The reviewer, Felicity O'Dell, writes about alphabetical order, the different types of entries, problems in English usage etc. Using references she criticizes the new book for its lack of attention to 'prepositions' but balances this with praise for its entries on 'functions' and 'style'.

▶ TASK 84

1 Read the text below and identify the points raised above.

2 Can you identify any other relevant evaluative comments?

3 Ask yourself what criteria the reviewer used to make these comments.

4 Would you find the comments (and criteria) useful in deciding whether this book is worth buying?

There are different types of entries. There are, for example, those which simply explain grammar terms like 'person', 'conjunction' or 'case'. Then there are those which deal with such aspects of grammar as 'negative words and sentences', 'present perfect' and 'non-finite clauses'. Then there are some entries which explain particular problems in English usage, covering, for instance, such points as 'bring and take', 'quite and rather' and 'either'. In this category could be included the entries on different individual prepositions but, on the whole, this category is given much less attention than in *Practical English Usage*. More extensive than in Swan there is, however, a group of entries considering different functions in English from 'advising' through 'inviting' and 'thanking' to 'warning'. Finally, there are a number of entries dealing with broader aspects of style such as 'letter-writing', 'formal and informal English', 'punctuation' and 'polite and not polite'. One could probably include the entry on 'sex' in this category too!

In the next part of the review the layout (including the illustrations) is examined:

The *A-Z* is attractive to look at with well-spaced entries making use of varied typefaces, boxes, diagrams and also line drawings to clarify points wherever possible. There is, for example, a useful picture illustrating a number of place prepositions on page 363. There are cartoons to show the use of different exclamations – 'Oh dear! How terrible! He's drowning,' for instance. Entries are fully cross-referenced, notes on register are provided where appropriate and common errors are indicated with a line through them. At the end of the book there is an *A-Z* of irregular verbs and an alphabetical list of the 600 or so entries in the book.

▶ **TASK 85**

1 In the above extract decide whether the reviewer is making positive or negative comments about the book.

2 List the layout items mentioned in the review that you would find important and useful, for example the cross-references.

In a similar way to the findings of other types of evaluation the reviewer then makes some personal and considered comments about the book. She starts from the point of view of the teacher and then refers to her experience of learners' needs in grammar books. She points out that they often like to have grammar reference books accompanied by exercises. She then focuses on the written language in the book which she thinks might be too academic for post intermediate/pre-advanced students. Its accessibility for teachers is also considered in comparison with Leech's other grammar books.

As a language teacher I find most language reference books fascinating and this one is no exception. The introduction to the book says that it is aimed at both learners and teachers. Learners, however, in my experience, prefer grammar reference books with accompanying exercises and there are a number of excellent and popular ones on the market at the moment. If an exercise book is not wanted by the student then *An A-Z of English Grammar and Usage,* as previously mentioned, bears certain resemblances to Michael Swan's *Practical English Usage* and the latter book seems to me to be written in language which any pre-advanced learner will find more accessible. Teachers themselves may well prefer to use a more academic grammar, such as one of Leech's own, although the *A-Z* may well prove useful both as an interesting book to dip into and as a clarifier of certain points.

(EFL Gazette 122:22)

► TASK 86

Read the above extracts of O'Dell's review. You may find information in **2.4** above useful before answering these questions:

1 Do you have enough information in the review to make a personal judgement on the book?

2 With reference to your teaching situation, what further information would you require to decide whether to buy the book or not?

10.3 Summary

As was pointed out earlier, book reviews are useful for practitioners to make some initial judgements about materials, either for personal use or class work. The above review focuses on evaluation in the workplan stage and less on the aspects of the grammar book in actual classroom use. These two stages in the materials evaluation process are explored further in Section Three below.

11 Teacher evaluation

11.1 Introduction

There are two perspectives on the nature of teacher evaluation. The first is associated with evaluation of teachers, primarily for purposes of appraisal. According to this view, evaluation is used as a means to examine teachers. The second perspective takes up the formative nature of evaluation where evaluation is used as a means to develop teachers' skills. The examining role is considered first.

11.2 Grading teachers: context and aim

As part of the requirements for the award of the Diploma in the Teaching of English as a Foreign Language (DTEFLA), candidates are assessed in two ways: a written examination and a practical. For the practical, candidates are observed teaching two different lessons to classes of different levels, one of which must be an elementary class. The aim of the teaching practice sessions is to provide the trainee teachers with an opportunity to demonstrate their competence in the classroom.

11.3 Design and procedures

Before the observation, assessors normally have a brief discussion with the trainees so that they get an idea of what they should expect to see, and they usually ask for a copy of the lesson plan for the class they will observe. There may also be a brief follow-up discussion after the lesson.

Assessors complete an assessment form (see **2.5**, 'Grading teachers') for the assessment of the trainees. They are instructed not to 'be actively involved in any way in the lesson' (RSA/UCLES:27).

▶ TASK 87

1 What do you perceive as the primary purpose of this evaluation?
2 What do you think are the drawbacks of observing only one or two demonstration lessons?
3 In what ways do you think that the trainees themselves could be involved in the evaluation process? Give details.

The next example demonstrates ways in which trainees may take an active part in their own evaluations. In doing so, they move towards a formative evaluation which has as its primary purpose the aim of teacher self-development.

11.4 Teacher evaluation: self-development

A different approach to teacher evaluation is provided by the work of Williams (1989). In particular, her work addresses the role of developmental, as opposed to judgemental, observations in in-service training.

11.5 The context

The context for Williams' work is in-service training for primary school teachers in Singapore. Her work challenges assumptions about 'good' and 'bad' teaching such as:

'... observers can tell what is 'good' and 'bad' in a classroom according to some prescribed checklist ... telling teachers what they are doing 'right' and 'wrong' will in fact lead to better teaching ...'
(Williams 1989:85)

▶ TASK 88

What do you think are some of the disadvantages associated with a 'traditional' approach to classroom observations, i.e. where a teacher 'performs' in front of a trainer who sits at the back of a class ticking items on a checklist (see 2.5)?

Traditionally it is the trainer/observer who leads the reporting back on a lesson. The teacher's role is to listen and then to try and 'get it right' next time. Williams (1989:86) rejects this approach as unsuitable for the following reasons:

1 It is threatening, frightening, and regarded as an ordeal.
2 The teacher has no responsibility for the evaluation; it is trainer-centred.
3 It is prescriptive.
4 The checklists try to cover too much at once.
5 There is unlikely to be continuity from visit to visit, and the visits themselves may not be linked to a specific course.
6 It is not participant-centred with individual pacing or choices.

▶ TASK 89
Go through the list above and suggest ways in which to reduce or
eliminate the problems mentioned.

11.6 Aims

The aim of the evaluation was largely to develop an alternative training
methodology for classroom visits: one that is 'participant-centred, and
allows for the teacher's own decisions and choices' (1989:86). Williams
emphasizes the importance of observations that encourage the involvement of the classroom teachers' themselves where they, as opposed to the
external trainer/inspector, develop an understanding about their classes:
description, explanation, and evaluation. The aim is to use evaluation as a
means for teachers to work towards self-development.

11.7 Design and procedures

Self-evaluation questionnaires
Four phases may be identified with the classroom observations:

1 pre-observation preparation/discussion
2 the observation itself
3 teacher reflection on the observation
4 post-observation discussion

This whole process is guided by a questionnaire to be used by both trainer
and trainee, as follows:

Before the lesson, look at your plan and ask yourself:
1 Have you chosen an activity that is interesting and will generate meaningful language use?

2 What classroom arrangement will you use? What materials do you need?

3 Is your organization smooth? Are the instructions clear? Do the pupils know the 'rules' of
   your class (who they can talk to, when, etc.)?

4 At what point in your lesson will the pupils use language for a real purpose?

5 Write down a question you will ask to encourage a *thoughtful* answer rather than a *correct*
   answer.

**During the lesson and after the lesson, ask yourself these questions and write the
answers:**
1 Write down something(s) that a pupil said in the lesson where language was used for a
   purpose.

2 Write down any evidence that your activity was successful/unsuccessful, was smoothly/
   badly organized, was interesting/boring.

3 Who was not involved? Why?

4 Which question provided a thoughtful answer? Write down your question

My thoughts:
What would you like to improve/have done better in the lesson? What have you learnt? Write
down your thoughts about how you would like to improve/change/develop your teaching in
the future.

(Williams 1989:88)

The questions before the lesson provide the teachers with a checklist to help plan the lesson. These are also discussed in a pre-observation session with the trainer. During the lesson, the trainer joins a group of learners, contributes where appropriate, and gathers data 'rather than judgements' (Williams 1989:89) about what is happening in the class. After the lesson, the teacher completes the remaining parts of the questionnaire which, together with the data gathered by the trainer, provides the focus for the follow-up to the observation session.

Visits

There are three visits integrated within the in-service course. The first takes place early on and is intended both to support the teacher and to encourage cooperative work between trainer and teacher.

The second visit has a different focus; it concentrates on what the teacher has learned on the course. This is reflected in the design of the second self-evaluation form:

Before the lesson ask yourself:
Is your activity at an appropriate intellectual level to stretch and challenge children of this age? Is it too easy/difficult? Is it interesting, motivating? Is there enough opportunity for the pupils to talk?

What meaningful language will it promote?

Where will there be opportunities for pupils to give their own ideas?

What is the place of the activity in your scheme of work? What preceded it? What will follow it? *Show this on your lesson plan.*

Show how it might involve/lead into reading, writing, grammar, etc.

What might the pupils learn? Write the aim of the activity and the language aims on your lesson plan.

What provision have you made for pupils who finish quickly/slowly?

During and after the lesson, ask yourself:
What evidence was there that the pupils were interested/not interested?

Who was not involved? Why?

Write down on paper some language that the pupils used. Was it meaningful or meaningless?

What will you do next to follow up this lesson?

Which of your aims were achieved? Were other things achieved instead?

When did pupils give their own ideas? Did you *accept* their ideas? Did they have a fair share of time to talk or did you dominate the discussion?

What have you learnt? Write down how you would like to develop your teaching in the future.

(Williams 1989:89)

This second self-evaluation form focuses more on specific factors and their explanations, for example: what evidence was there that the learners were interested or not interested? Who was not involved? Why?

After this second observation, teachers are then invited to work through a number of self-evaluation forms (on their own or with a colleague). Here is an example:

Do you ask meaningful and thought-provoking questions? Can you improve your questioning techniques? Why not try to analyse your questions yourself?

Before the lesson:
Write down a question that you will ask for each or some of these categories:

★ one that you don't know the answer to
★ one that is about the children themselves
★ one that encourages a lengthy rather than one-word answer
★ one that gets the children to think
★ one that asks for their opinion
★ one that starts a discussion.

How will you respond to their answers?

During the lesson:
Tape-record a part of your lesson, ask a colleague to write down some of your questions and the responses, or try to write them down yourself.

After the lesson:
Look at your questions. Decide whether they were meaningful or meaningless. Which of the above categories did they fall into? Which questions did you think were the best? Why?

Ask your colleague which question he/she liked best and why?

Did you give the pupils enough time to think of a reply?

Did you try to involve all the pupils or only the chosen few?

Did you need to repeat or rephrase any questions? Why?

Look at your response to the children's replies. Which showed real interest in the replies? Which were simply judgemental ('good', 'no', etc.)? Did you accept their thoughts or impose your own?

What have you learnt?

(Williams 1989:90)

▶ **TASK 90**

Identify the different ways in which:

1 cooperation between teacher and trainer is encouraged

2 the teachers are more involved in the evaluation process than in 'traditional' classroom evaluation visits.

The third visit is the one where evaluative judgements are made. Williams (1989:90) explains that 'This is a requirement imposed on the programme'. Again, a questionnaire may be used, or the trainer and teacher team up and devise their own questions. Similar procedures to the previous visits are followed. Additionally, the trainer makes notes for the teacher that may include general comments on strengths or points to think about for self-development. The trainer communicates these thoughts to the teacher in the form of a letter.

11.8 Evaluation of the evaluation

An evaluation of this 'new' approach to teacher self-development was carried out by means of a questionnaire. Williams (1989:91) describes the results as 'positive': the visits were rated as 'helpful/useful', and appropriate in number (78 out of 110), and most of the teachers (101 out of 106) felt able to continue with the self-evaluation after the course. However, teachers still reported a sense of anxiety before the observations.

▶ TASK 91

1 In what ways do you think that nervousness before the classroom observations can be reduced/eliminated?

2 In what ways could these teacher evaluation procedures be implemented in your own context? How would you modify them?

11.9 Summary

In the first example, evaluation was primarily for purposes of accountability where a summative judgement is made of a trainee's teaching ability. Further, in terms of the evaluation framework (see **4.2**), the evaluation criteria are prescribed by the external assessment agency which does not involve the trainee teacher in the evaluation process. The information derived from the evaluation is expressed in terms of a Distinction, Pass, or Fail, and is not intended in any formal way to feed into the teacher self-development process.

The procedures in the second example describe an approach to teacher self-evaluation through developmental classroom observations. Over a period of time, teachers are encouraged to describe, explain, and evaluate their own classroom practices and to engage in self-evaluation, either individually or in pairs. It is intended that teachers will gain control of their own personal development using the process of evaluation.

12   Evaluating learner outcomes: product

12.1 Introduction

We shall discuss two different approaches to assessing learner performance. The first to be considered is the IELTS (International English
Language Testing Service).

12.2 The context and aims

This is a proficiency examination designed primarily for candidates wishing to study at institutions of higher education in the UK and Australia.
Examination results are intended to reflect the suitability of candidates in
terms of their overall language proficiency for training through the
medium of English. As such, the design and the content of the examination cannot relate to any particular language learning syllabus.

The IELTS is divided into four subtests, two of which are based on topics
of general interest (Listening and Speaking); the others (Reading and
Writing) are specialized in topic orientation to reflect the academic background of the candidate's course of study.

12.3 Procedure

The examination has been developed by the British Council, the International Development Program of Australian Universities and Colleges, and
the University of Cambridge Local Examinations Syndicate. The
individual subtests vary in length and are taken in the following order:

Reading	55 minutes
Writing	45 minutes
Listening	30 minutes
Speaking	11–15 minutes

12.4 Examination results

The results are reported in the form of nine band scores, on a scale of 0–9.
These are described as follows:

The nine Academic Bands and their descriptive statements are as follows:

9 Expert User. Has fully operational command of the language: appropriate, accurate and fluent with complete understanding.

8 Very Good User. Has full operational command of the language with only occasional unsystematic inaccuracies and inappropriacies. Misunderstandings may occur in unfamiliar situations. Handles complex detailed argumentation well.

7 Good User. Has operational command of the language, though with occasional inaccuracies, inappropriacies and misunderstandings in some situations. Generally handles complex language well and understands detailed reasoning.

6 Competent User. Has generally effective command of the language despite some inaccuracies, inappropriacies and misunderstandings. Can use and understand fairly complex language, particularly in familiar situations.

5 Modest User. Has partial command of the language, coping with overall meaning in most situations, though is likely to make many mistakes. Should be able to handle basic communication in own field.

4 Limited User. Basic competence is limited to familiar situations. Has frequent problems in understanding and expression. Is not able to use complex language.

3 Extremely Limited User. Conveys and understands only general meaning in very familiar situations. Frequent breakdowns in communication occur.

2 Intermittent User. No real communication is possible except for the most basic information using isolated words or short formulae in familiar situations and to meet immediate needs. Has great difficulty understanding spoken and written English.

1 Non User. Essentially has no ability to use the language beyond possibly a few isolated words.

0 Did not attempt the test. No assessable information.

(An Introduction to IELTS:6)

Although there may be variation across institutions, a minimum average score of Band 6 or 6.5 (on the four subtests) is typically required. For linguistically demanding academic courses, it is recommended that a candidate obtains at least 7, preferably 7.5, whereas for linguistically less exacting training courses a band level of 5 or 5.5 is suggested.

▶   ## TASK 92

Compare the ways in which results are reported on two proficiency tests; use the IELTS bands above and these TOEFL results:

TOEFL SCALED SCORES				Month	Year	Centre number	Sponsor code	Mo/Day/Year	
Section 1	Section 2	Section 3	Total score	Test date				Date of birth	Sex
50	55	52	523	SEP	90	XXX	XXX	10/05/70	M

Institution code	Dept. code
XXXX	XX
XXXX	XX
XXXX	XX

See other side
for explanation

	Native country
	JAPAN
	Native language
	JAPANESE

Reason for taking TOEFL	Degree	TOEFL taken before
1	2	1

TOEFL SCORE COMPARISON TABLE
(based on the scores of 875,897 examinees
who took the test from July 1987 through June 1989)

		SECTION SCORES					
TOTAL SCORE		Section 1		Section 2		Section 3	
Your score	% Lower than you	Your score	% Lower than you	Your score	% Lower than you	Your score	% Lower than you
660	99	66	98	66	97	66	99
640	97	64	95	64	94	64	96
620	93	62	91	62	91	62	92
600	88	60	86	60	85	60	87
580	81	58	79	58	77	58	80
560	73	56	72	56	70	56	71
540	62	54	62	54	59	54	60
520	51	52	52	52	49	52	50
500	39	50	42	50	39	50	39
480	29	48	31	48	30	48	30
460	20	46	22	46	23	46	22
440	13	44	14	44	16	44	16
420	8	42	8	42	11	42	11
400	5	40	4	40	7	40	7
380	2	38	2	38	4	38	4
360	1	36	1	36	2	36	3
340		34	1	34	1	34	2
320		32		32	1	32	1
300		30		30		30	

(TOEFL: Score table)

12.5 Feedback

We have seen above how the band descriptors can help receiving institutions of higher education to select students. However, another of the aims of the IELTS is to provide feedback to candidates who take this examination. The following information is provided to candidates (*An Introduction to IELTS*:6):

'Experience has shown that the speed of learning, as expressed by the number of hours required to improve one band, can vary from person to person between 100 and over 200 hours, with a tendency for more rapid rates of progress at the lower levels.'

▶ TASK 93

To what extent would you find the feedback in the information above useful from the point of view of:

1 teachers hoping to help learners pass the IELTS?

2 learners wishing to improve on their scores?

12.6 Summary

This proficiency examination focuses generally on learner outcomes in terms of products. Since the bands are related to proficiency levels, and not to a specific class syllabus, the IELTS does not provide any detailed information on what candidates who have obtained a low score need to do in order to improve on their performance, i.e. band level. It is thus a summative measure of what learners can do, providing limited guidance in the area of the four language skills where students need to improve their language proficiency.

The second example below, by way of contrast with IELTS, represents an approach where learner evaluation is integrated within classroom language learning.

13 Evaluating learner outcomes: process

13.1 The context

The evaluation of learner outcomes in terms of the process of learning is discussed here with reference to the Primary Language Record (henceforth PLR). This approach arose from a need felt by many different professionals (teachers and head teachers, in-service staff, members of the inspectorate) for an improved means of recording in the classroom children's progress in the area of language development. The PLR was researched and designed in schools in London, for use with learners for whom English is a mother tongue or a second language.

13.2 Aims

The aims of the PLR are described as follows (Preface):

'to inform and guide other teachers who do not yet know the child; to inform the head teacher and others in positions of responsibility about the child's work; to provide parents with information and assessment of the child's progress. But, in addition, the PLR is also based on the principle of the need for records to support and inform the day-to-day teaching in the classroom.'
(Barrs, Ellis, Hester, and Thomas 1988)

13.3 Design and procedures

The design of the PLR centres around the following principles:

- the involvement of parents
- the involvement of learners
- the involvement of all teachers who teach the children
- the importance of recording children's progress in other community languages they know as well as in English
- the importance of recording developments across the curriculum in all major language modes
- the importance of a clear framework for evaluating progress in language.

The PLR is divided into three parts:

Part A is completed during the first term at school. Here is an example:

Part A To be completed during the Autumn Term

A1 Record of discussion between child's parent(s) and class teacher *(Handbook pages 12-13)*

At home T. uses both Kurdish and English (dad lipreads English, mum lipreads mostly Kurdish). He speaks both languages equally fluently. Although both his parents are deaf, they have a phone at home; grandma rings T. and he passes on the message to mum or dad in English or Kurdish and sign language. He loves watching TV and puts it on himself. He also likes watching videos, especially Sumo wrestling cartoons and Fireman Sam. He also loves quiz games, anything with letters in. Grandma says he learned his alphabet from the television. He writes and draws a lot at home and plays with his sister.

Signed Parent(s) _____   Teacher _____

Date _27·2·89·_____

A2 Record of language/literacy conference with child *(Handbook pages 14-15)*

T. says he likes watching television, especially 'the Incredible Hulk', 'Thundercats', 'Sumo wrestling' 'but that's not on TV any more so I took home a book from the library on Sumo'. He also enjoys watching quiz games like 'Countdown' and 'Blockbusters'. His favourite book at present is 'Fireman Sam', but he also likes 'Thomas the Tank Engine' and 'Biff and Chip.'

He likes playing with his toys especially spaceships, and going out in the garden. He says he plays with his little sister, which she likes, but not when he pretends to be the Hulk and scares her. He likes cooking with mum too.

© CLPE/ILEA 1988, 1989

(Barrs et al. 1990:45)

As shown above, Part A consists of an initial administrative section followed by the record of the discussion with parents (A1) and the learner (A2).

Part B is completed during the second term. This concerns the learner as a 'language user' and has separate subsections devoted to talking and listening (B1), reading (B2), and writing (B3). Here is an example:

Part B
To be completed during the Spring Term and to include information from all teachers currently teaching the child.

Child as a language user (one or more languages)
(Handbook pages 17-18)

Teachers should bear in mind the Authority's Equal Opportunities Policies (race, gender and class) in completing each section of the record and should refer to *Educational Opportunities for All?*, the ILEA report on special educational needs.

B1 Talking and listening
(Handbook pages 19-22)

Please comment on the child's development and use of spoken language in different social and curriculum contexts, in English and/or other community languages: evidence of talk for learning and thinking; range and variety of talk for particular purposes; experience and confidence in talking and listening with different people in different settings.

M's confidence in speaking has increased greatly since I have known her. She is much more willing to put forward her ideas, especially in small-group activities, and tends not to just copy others now. She is a good listener and loves listening to stories. She can always paraphrase a story. M. is able to order her thoughts well and makes good use of her vocabulary.

What experiences and teaching have helped/would help development in this area? Record outcomes of any discussion with head teacher, other staff, or parent(s).

M. is earning more and more respect from peers who now take more notice of her ideas. These conversational qualities are her strength in language work; this increase in respect will boost her confidence. Therefore it is important that she is given the opportunities to practise her spoken language across the curriculum.

B2 Reading
(Handbook pages 23-28)

Please comment on the child's progress and development as a reader in English and/or other community languages: the stage at which the child is operating (refer to the reading scales on pages 26-27); the range, quantity and variety of reading in all areas of the curriculum; the child's pleasure and involvement in story and reading, alone or with others; the range of strategies used when reading and the child's ability to reflect critically on what is read.

M's attitude towards reading is more positive now. She is keen to learn, having overcome the fact that most pupils in the class can read better than her. Previously she would not read for fear that others would find out she had difficulties. She almost knows her initial sounds and is just becoming aware that these sounds are linked to the beginning of words. She is operating at reading scale 2, stage 1. M. is focusing primarily on the print. She has 1:1 correspondence and recognition of certain words. She also makes use of picture cues.

What experiences and teaching have helped/would help development in this area? Record outcomes of any discussion with head teacher, other staff, or parent(s).

M. needs simply-constructed reading books with enough content to stimulate and interest her. She also needs opportunities for shared reading and 1:1 reading with an adult.

(Barrs et al. 1990:45)

The final section, Part C, is completed in the final term. This is used for additional information on the learner's language progress, such that the record is as up to date as possible. Here is an example:

Part C   To be completed during the Summer Term*

C1 Comments on the record by child's parent(s)

Her reading has improved greatly. She is thrilled to be able to read to her brother — he still has to tell her a few words occasionally but she's delighted to be able to read well enough for him to pay attention. Her spelling is improving now that she is interested in it.

C2 Record of language/literacy conference with child

"Sometimes when I'm reading I need help with a word if I don't understand it. I like reading best at bed-time because I can concentrate, and reading stories to my brother. I enjoy reading at school but only when it's quiet, not when people come and disturb me. My best bit of writing was the one I did with B. We had the same title, we chose it together, then we went off and wrote our own stories. When we had finished we found we both had Chipmunks in it. B. writes fast so she finished before me but she still had to put in commas and full stops, but I write slowly and do them as I go along and it takes a long time."

C3 Information for receiving teacher
This section is to ensure that information for the receiving teacher is as up to date as possible. Please comment on changes and development in any aspect of the child's language since Part B was completed.

G. has started to see reading as something rewarding and satisfying. I think it's because she is able to choose her own reading material, which she enjoys doing. In the past couple of weeks she has really taken on board that writing can be fun and interesting, and has worked very well. She works quite well in small groups. She has become a moderately fluent reader on reading scale 1.

What experiences and teaching have helped/would help development? Record outcomes of any discussion with head teacher, other staff, or parent(s).

Her reading could improve if she didn't always 'play safe' in her choice of books, so perhaps encourage her to choose a wider range of reading material. After talking to her mother we agreed that she would appreciate and benefit from writing her stories on the computer as it might make it quicker for her to get her thoughts onto paper.

Signed: Parent(s) _____   Class Teacher _____

Date _____   Head Teacher _____

*To be completed by the Summer half-term for 4th year juniors.

(*Barrs et al. 1988:35*)

▶ TASK 94

What do you think are the strengths and weaknesses of the PLR approach to evaluating learners?

13.4 Summary

Examinations such as the IELTS (see **12**), and records and profiles of learner achievements, are designed in response to particular evaluation needs. The IELTS certainly goes beyond the mere reporting of a test score but is incomplete in terms of a profile of achievement. However, this latter dimension does not reflect a primary aim of this type of test.

The PLR, on the other hand, is an example of a classroom evaluation procedure that gathers information over time, working towards a comprehensive profile of a learner's progress and achievements. In contrast to the IELTS, the PLR focuses on the process of learning with a view to informing the teaching and learning process. It is thus formative in purpose. Further, by involving parents and learners in addition to the teacher, the PLR is far more likely to be a reliable and valid record of a learner's strengths and weaknesses than a measure which takes information from one source (i.e. the learner) and does this in a one-off, two-hour pencil and paper test. Although the PLR has been developed for the ESL teaching and learning context in England, the principles guiding its design and the formative information on learner progress that it yields is clearly generalizable across other contexts and other languages.

The next and final evaluation also makes use of a test. But like the Spada evaluation (see **6**), the test is not used for monitoring language development over time as in the case of the PLR. What is interesting about this next evaluation (Lawrence 1990) is that it makes use of a variety of procedures in evaluating the extent to which teachers actually do what is expected of them by their national curriculum.

14   Syllabus evaluation

14.1 Introduction

The final example reported in this Section is in the area of syllabus evaluation. It is important because it illustrates several procedures for evaluation that we identified earlier in the book (see **3.3** and **3.4**). This evaluation was carried out at the University of Zambia (Lawrence 1990) and focuses on the methodology used to teach the sentence patterns that are incorporated in the revised structure component of the English syllabus taught at Grade 8 level in Zambian Junior–Secondary schools.

14.2 The context

In Zambia, the medium of instruction in primary and secondary schools is English. English is also the official language of the country but not the mother tongue. A few years ago, a revised English language syllabus that aimed to take the needs of the learners into account was introduced. The objectives of this syllabus emphasized the teaching of language *use*. This evaluation examined the effectiveness of the classroom implementation of the structure component of the syllabus which was intended to be oriented towards the communicative use of language.

14.3 Aims

The main aims of this evaluation relate to the following four questions:

1 What is the proficiency level of pupils in Grade 8 classes?

2 Does the Grade 8 syllabus adequately respond to the immediate needs of pupils to study effectively through English-medium education in Junior–Secondary schools?

3 Does the structure syllabus do what it sets out to do, as indicated in the official Syllabus Handbook?

4 What improvements could be made to the existing syllabus in areas such as syllabus design, syllabus content, methodology, and teacher education? What form might these improvements take?

▶ TASK 95

If you were given the above terms of reference for this evaluation, how would you describe the evaluation?

Is there an emphasis on:
a) product objectives?
b) process objectives?
c) formative evaluation?
d) summative evaluation?

14.4 Design and procedures

Introduction

This evaluation (Lawrence 1990) uses an essentially ethnographic model because it is concerned with analysing and describing current classroom practices, focusing not only on what the teacher is doing, but also on what the learner is doing.

The following four evaluation procedures were used by Lawrence:

1 proficiency tests (administered to Grade 8 pupils)
2 a questionnaire (given to a sample of over one hundred practising teachers)
3 classroom observation (twenty-six Grade 8 structure lessons)
4 structured interviews (with Grade 8 teachers).

Design

The overall design of the evaluation was as follows. A proficiency test, based on Grade 8 textbooks and readers, was designed. This, in addition to the results from parts of the National Grade 7 examinations, was used by Lawrence to analyse the proficiency level of pupils entering Secondary school. She looked at the ability of the pupils to work in an English-medium curriculum, using the test results as one criterion to evaluate whether the syllabus was appropriate to the pupils' actual ability to use language in other curriculum areas.

Structure lessons were observed in order to inform the design of the questionnaire and the classroom observation schedule. In terms of the sequence of the evaluation procedures, the classroom observation was carried out first so as not to interfere with how the teachers worked in their classrooms. This was then followed by the questionnaire and the interview. In the structured interview, Lawrence was able to clarify points arising from the lessons observed.

To describe the structure lessons, four pairs of criteria were used:

– analytic and synthetic (Wilkins 1976)
– cognitive and mechanical
– inductive and deductive
– use and usage (Widdowson 1978)

These are explained as follows:

An analytic approach to teaching and learning is one where the learner is helped to become familiar with language beyond the sentence, developing the ability to use and understand written texts and spoken discourse. A synthetic approach, on the other hand, deals with language as isolated elements and sentences.

Cognitive and mechanical are criteria related to the analytic and synthetic dimensions: skill using fluency activities such as information sharing or role play will involve the cognitive use of language, whereas mechanical use refers to activities such as controlled drilling.

An inductive approach to structure teaching is one where there is no explicit initial rule teaching. This contrasts with a deductive approach where there is explicit teaching of grammar rules.

The usage or use distinction reflects two aspects of performance: the former is defined as the ability to compose correct sentences, which manifests the user's knowledge of the language system; the latter as the ability to use that knowledge of the language system in order to achieve some communicative purpose.

Lawrence emphasizes that the teachers in the evaluation study were at no point aware that these particular features were being analysed. She further stresses that the findings in relation to the above criteria are taken

'to indicate tendency for one feature to be emphasized, not necessarily at the expense of the other . . . What emerges from the analysis is therefore a suggestion of characteristic tendencies in an approach to teaching structure.'
(Lawrence 1990)

The tests
The proficiency test was administered to two hundred pupils in ten secondary schools (boys and girls) within the Zambian state school system. This included both urban and rural schools.

▶ **TASK 96**
What do you think of this procedure as a means of evaluating pupils?

The questionnaire
The aim of the questionnaire was to find out the teacher's perceptions of how they actually implement the structure syllabus, by identifying the main features of a structure lesson.

▶ TASK 97

If you wanted to analyse the ways in which teachers approached the teaching of a structure lesson, what questions would you put to the teachers concerned?

These are sample questions from the questionnaire used by Lawrence (1990):

---

1 *When your pupils use a 'local form' of English (e.g. cope up with/monthend), which of the following approaches do you use most frequently? (N = never, R = rarely, S = sometimes, O = often, NA = nearly always)*

	N	R	S	O	NA
a) tell pupils it is an error and do correction work on the item					
b) say that it is wrong to use it in written work only					
c) say that it is all right to use it when speaking to Zambians					
d) say that it is all right to use it in speaking and writing at any time					

2 *Which one of the following ways do you use to select structures to teach?*

	N	R	S	O	NA
a) use a diagnostic test (a written exercise) before teaching an item in the syllabus?					
b) choose structures pupils use incorrectly in compositions?					
c) follow a Departmental scheme of work?					
d) Try to teach all the structures in the Grade 8 syllabus?					

If you wish, give reasons for your answer to 2:

....

3 *Below are a few ways in which to introduce a structure lesson. Indicate how frequently you use each one:*

	N	R	S	O	NA
a) ask pupils to chorus an oral drill, or dia-logue repeating a new structure?					
b) tell a story using the structure repeatedly, followed by questions?					
c) use actions, pictures, objects to convey the meaning of a structure?					
d) give pupils a rule explanation with model sentences to illustrate it?					
e) give pupils a passage to read in which the structure is used together with a number of other structures?					

4 *Which one of the following approaches to rule explanation do you use most frequently?*
(Tick one box)

a) give pupils a simple rule explanation with
   model sentence at the beginning of a lesson?   ☐

b) ask pupils to explain a rule after they have
   practised using a structure?   ☐

c) leave out rule explanations and rely only on
   oral and written practice using the structure?   ☐

If you wish to give reasons for your answer to 4, add here: ....

....

(Lawrence 1990)

▶ TASK 98

Can you suggest ways in which teachers could collaborate with an external evaluator to write questions for a questionnaire designed to illuminate an aspect of classroom practice?

Since the questionnaire in this evaluation focused on what teachers do when presenting and practising language in the classroom, Lawrence developed the questionnaire in conjunction with a group of experienced teachers studying at the University of Zambia. She first drafted the questionnaire and then tried it out on this group, revising questions in the light of their comments. These teachers then administered the questionnaire themselves in their own provinces. Afterwards, the questionnaires and responses were returned to the evaluator for further modification. Lawrence (1990) comments that changes mostly concerned 'the wording of questions and rubrics, the addition of choices, and changes to the type of format for responses'.

Classroom observation
Eight of the ten schools used for the proficiency testing took part in the classroom observations. The observations were undertaken by Lawrence at the presentation, practice, and production stages of structure lessons in the following manner:

1 Relevant information was recorded on an open-ended data sheet divided into four ten-minute sessions;
2 The lessons were also audio-recorded and transcribed for analysis of the verbal interaction in the classroom;
3 The classroom observations (using the same criteria as the questionnaire) were analysed immediately after each lesson. Using these open-ended data sheets and recordings the dominant features of the lesson were determined.

A sample observation of a teacher in a structure lesson follows:

Minutes	SY	DED	COG	USG	PC	No. of pupil responses (N=28)
1–10	+	+	+	+	L/S	9
11–21	+	+	+	+	L/S	10
22–32	–	n/a	+	–	L/S/W	7
33–40	–	n/a	+	+	W/R	–

SY	= synthetic	USG	= usage
DED	= deductive	PC	= performance channel
COG	= cognitive	n/a	= not applicable

Table 6 (*Lawrence 1990*)

Information of this kind, which provides an overall indication of the methodology teachers actually used when teaching structure, was subsequently compared with the answers from the questionnaire which reveal the teachers' perceptions of their classroom strategies. Together these data provide an indication of the overall patterns adopted in the teaching of structure in Grade 8 classes.

Structured interviews
This was the final step in the investigation into how the syllabus was being implemented. Fifteen Grade 8 teachers were interviewed privately in a suitable room in each school. The responses were recorded on interview sheets.

An extract from the structured interview follows:

1 What helps you to decide what method to use in a structure lesson? Is it:
   – teacher training?
   – available material?
   – other teachers?
   – Head of Department?
   – other reasons?

2 When you teach a structure, do you think you teach the form more than the actual use of the structure in a structure lesson?

3 In a structure lesson, what do you do when your pupil makes an error:
   a) orally?
   b) in written practice?

4 Do you feel it is necessary to correct all errors made in a structure lesson? If not, what is the basis for your selection of errors to correct?

▶ TASK 99

Four different evaluation procedures were used in this study. What do you consider to be the advantages and disadvantages of the procedures adopted by Lawrence?

14.5 Findings

With reference to the aims of the evaluation (see **14.3**) three of the main findings are:

1 The level of the pupils' overall proficiency was lower than expected. A significant number of them did not reach the level required for studying through the medium of English.
2 There was evidence that the syllabus did not respond to the actual need of the pupils to follow an English–medium curriculum.
3 The methodology adopted by many of the teachers was in contrast with that advocated by the revised structure syllabus.

These points are considered further below.

Tests
The findings from the administration of the proficiency tests indicate that a substantial number of pupils have problems in dealing with the English used in some Grade 8 textbooks in different school subjects. In other words, the evaluation revealed that a number of pupils do not have an adequate level of English to learn their other school subjects through the medium of English.

Questionnaires, observation, interviews
The findings from these three evaluation procedures revealed similar information. The main approaches used to teach structure, as practised by the Grade 8 teachers in this evaluation, were as follows:

deductive   usage   synthetic   cognitive

▶ TASK 100

Consider the four features of the structure lesson given above (see also the criteria described in **14.4**). What do these mean to you in terms of actual classroom practice, i.e. the approach used by teachers to teach grammar?

Lawrence's evaluation shows us that teachers favoured a methodology where grammar is taught explicitly, with a focus on knowledge about language at the level of the single sentence. The cognitive element did not arise from a problem-solving type of language learning activity in which pupils are invited to participate, but was reflected in the predominance of rule teaching.

The approaches revealed as least favoured by teachers in the structure lesson were:

mechanical   use   analytic

▶ TASK 101

In terms of classroom practice and the structure lesson, how would you interpret this last set of findings?

In summary, Lawrence provides evidence that the teaching focus in grammar lessons is still on language elements divorced from communicative language use. Importantly, she discovered that although many of the teachers thought they were teaching *use* of language, this was not mirrored in many instances by their actual classroom practice.

14.6 Feedback

In a context where English is used as the medium to learn school subjects, it is crucial that the teaching of English as a subject develops pupils' abilities to use the language effectively. The evaluation concludes that because of the Grade 8 pupils' need to use English fluently in other subjects, the present English language structure syllabus (where the actual focus in lessons is on form and not use as demonstrated by the subjects in this study) is not the most appropriate (Lawrence 1990:vi). As Lawrence explains:

'The concentration on synthetic-structural teaching leads to an emphasis on accuracy rather than fluency in the structure lesson (although the syllabus objectives emphasise use). The type of lesson leads to learner passivity and teacher control.'

(Lawrence 1990:vi–vii)

A number of implications for future action arise from this evaluation.

▶ TASK 102

What recommendations would you want to make in the light of the evaluation findings presented in **14.5**? (You may also find it useful to refer to **14.4**.)

In the field of teacher education, there would appear to be a case for in-service courses to work towards improving the implementation of the revised syllabus. One aim might be to increase teachers' awareness about their own classroom practice so that they would appreciate, for example, that they were not implementing the recommendation in the revised syllabus that rule teaching be kept to a minimum or teaching the *use* of

English, but still concentrating on formal accuracy as in the earlier syllabus. A second aim might be to develop the teachers' skills in providing their pupils with appropriate opportunities to practice language freely and naturally.

As far as syllabus development is concerned, recommendations could justifiably be made for changes that would involve a greater use of tasks that develop pupils' fluency in the use of English and, importantly, that these tasks be related to language needs across the curriculum in subjects such as history, geography, and mathematics.

14.7 Summary

The conclusions of the Lawrence evaluation study were that the structure syllabus was not appropriate to these learners' needs. Although the content of the structure syllabus was being implemented, it was not accompanied by a methodology appropriate to the development of language skills required by pupils who follow a curriculum through the medium of English. The findings from the evaluation have implications both for teacher self-development through in-service courses and for syllabus development. As such, this represents a formative evaluation of one component (i.e. the teaching and learning of structure) of a secondary school syllabus in a context where English is used as a Second Language.

In Section Two we examined fifteen case studies that relate to the evaluation of aspects of second or foreign language learning classrooms. Using an analysis of these studies, we have seen different approaches to the task of evaluating classrooms. We have also seen how important it is to gather qualitative as well as quantitative data, and the need to examine the processes of teaching and learning.

Exploring evaluation potential

15   General principles

15.1 Introduction

In this final section, we provide you with an opportunity to develop skills in designing evaluation procedures which can then be applied to a number of tasks where you are invited to plan evaluations relevant to your own teaching and learning contexts.

15.2 The framework for an evaluation

Evaluation should be planned systematically and based on certain principles. In **4.2** we put forward a summary of points that need to be addressed by anyone who wants to design an evaluation. In the following task, we recall some key questions by critically analysing the design of syllabus evaluations presented in Section Two.

▶ **TASK 103**

Aim
To analyse the basic design features of the CTP evaluation (see **5**) and the Lawrence evaluation (see **14**).

Resources
1 The framework presented in **4.2**.
2 The evaluation of the CTP presented in **5.2** to **5.6**.
3 The evaluation of the structure syllabus presented in **14.1** to **14.7**.

Procedures
1 Study the three resource documents.
2 Using these, go through the questions presented in the evaluation framework (see **4.2**) and draw up an outline of the CTP evaluation and the Lawrence study. You will need to decide which of the elements in the framework have been included and which have not.
3 Compare and contrast the two evaluation studies. Which one do you think is the more useful evaluation study? Give reasons for your answers.

4 With reference again to the questions in the evaluation framework (see **4.2**), consider other ways in which the evaluations could have been handled. For example, in your context, what would be the most appropriate way to undertake an evaluation of one of the components of your English language teaching syllabus? Give reasons for any suggestions you make.

16   Evaluation procedures

16.1 Planning evaluation procedures

It is important when undertaking evaluations to be able to select the appropriate procedures to collect the information you need. As we saw in Section One, there are a number of different techniques that we can use. These include questionnaires, observation sheets, checklists/inventories, interviews, and diaries. Since you need to be able to design your own evaluation tools, the next few tasks provide you with an opportunity to develop your skills in writing appropriate data-gathering instruments.

16.2 Writing items for a questionnaire

▶ TASK 104

Aim
To design appropriate items for a questionnaire.

Look at the Lawrence evaluation (see **14.1** to **14.7**), in particular at the questionnaire (see **14.4**) used to analyse the ways in which teachers taught their grammar lessons. Sample questions were given of those used in the questionnaire. However, no sample of questions about the procedures teachers used when giving oral or written practice within a structure lesson were given.

Context
As a starting point, here are two questions for a questionnaire designed to provide the information you need:

1 For *oral practice* in a structure lesson, which of the following do you use most frequently:
   a) (e.g. learners make up sentences from a substitution table?)
   b) . . .?

2 In *written practice* in a structure lesson which of the following exercises do you use most frequently:
   a) (e.g. learners fill in blanks or complete sentences?)
   b) . . .?

Procedures

1 Continue the lists for the two questions given above. Remember, it is important to relate your items to the specific context in which you would be evaluating the teaching of structure lessons.

2 Decide on the layout of your questions. Are you going to use the same one as Lawrence? Or are you going to try something different? Remember, it is important to use a format that is clear to those who will be answering your questions.

16.3 Self-evaluation questionnaire

▶ **TASK 105**

Aim

To draw up an inventory in order to evaluate approaches used in the teaching of vocabulary at three different stages of a lesson.

Procedures

1 For each of the three stages of a lesson write five statements you think reflect the way in which you teach vocabulary. The first statement is given as an example, but if it is inappropriate for you you may wish to change it.

	Yes	No
Stage One: Presentation		
1 I write new words on the blackboard.	___	___
2	___	___
3	___	___
4	___	___
Stage Two: Practice		
1 Learners use the new words in oral drills.	___	___
2	___	___
3	___	___
4	___	___
Stage Three: Production		
1 I use role play to consolidate use of new words.	___	___
2	___	___
3	___	___
4	___	___

2 Then, over a series of lessons, use these self-evaluation statements as a guide to analyse the ways in which you actually teach vocabulary.

3 Analyse your results. Do you actually do what you think you do when you teach vocabulary? Or do you use other methods?

4 What other scale could you use in place of 'Yes' or 'No'? Is there another way that may give you more information? As an example, what about a five point scale of some kind? (See **3.3** and **14.4** for alternatives.)

16.4 Observation sheets

▶ TASK 106

Aim
To design an appropriate observation sheet to evaluate the different question types used by teachers and learners.

Resources
You may find it useful to refer to observation schedules in **3.3, 6.4, 8.3,** and **14.4**.

Procedure
1 Consider the different question types that you think are used in classes and make a list of them.
2 Draw up an outline of an observation sheet which:
   a) compares the question types used by the learners and by the teacher(s);
   b) indicates how often these different questions types are used by (i) learners and (ii) the teacher.
3 Record one of your own lessons or arrange to observe one of your colleagues' lessons.
4 Complete the observation sheet while observing the lesson. If this is not possible, complete the observation sheet while listening to a recording of a lesson.
5 Was your observation sheet adequate? Or do you need to modify it to reflect accurately the types of questions used in class by both teachers and learners?

16.5 Preparing questions for an interview

▶ TASK 107

Aim
To write appropriate questions that you would ask teachers when interviewing them in order to find out about their classroom testing practices.

Context
There is to be a seminar on testing for teachers in your region and you have been asked to provide full details about how teachers in your region

use tests in their teaching. You decide to conduct interviews with teachers to discover if they use tests, and if they do, why. You also need to know when they test, and the content they test. You are also interested in the test formats they use, the criteria they use to mark their learners' work, and what they do with the results from the tests. Finally, you would like them to tell you about the problems they face when testing their learners.

Procedures

1 Write out a list of questions you would ask colleagues in order to find out the information listed above.

2 How many teachers do you think you would need to interview in order to get a balanced view of classroom testing in your region?

3 Now interview two or three of your colleagues using your interview questions. How useful were your questions? What changes would you need to make to them? Why?

Having briefly drawn up some procedures for gathering information in classrooms, we now invite you to apply these techniques to specific evaluation contexts. The emphasis in the tasks that follow is primarily on formative evaluation which can promote curriculum development and teacher self-development.

17 Evaluation of classroom methodology

The next tasks provide you with opportunities to evaluate aspects of classroom methodology. We start with ways in which errors are corrected in classroom (see **3.3** and **8**).

17.1 Error correction

▶ **TASK 108**

Aim
To evaluate the different methods a teacher uses to correct errors.

Resources
1 Lesson transcript (Miletto 1990):

(a) L: The . . .
(b) T: The . . .   The clothes are not Italian

(a) L: Thirty-two
(b) T: About thirty-two, I think . . .
(c) L: Thirty-five
(d) T: Say 'I think' . . . 'I think' . . .
(e) L: Near(,) under forty.
(f) T: 'I think' . . .
(g) L: I think thirty (,)-
(h) T: 'I think she's thirty-five.'
(i) L: I think she's thirty-five.

(a) L: I think she has, er, forty-three.
(b) T: She is. She's. She's.
(c) L: She's forty-three.

(a) L: I think she's a, she's a rich man wife.
(b) T: Did you understand? Say it again, didn't hear you.
(c) L: I think she's a rich man wife.
(d) T: A rich man's wife.

Procedures
After examining the extracts from the classroom transcript:

1 Decide what kind of errors were made.
2 Identify the methods the teacher used to correct these errors.
3 Comment on what took place.
4 Compare this teacher's error correction style with yours as described in 8.3, Task 76.

17.2 Presenting structure items

▶ TASK 109

Aim
To describe and evaluate how a teacher presents a structure item in class.

Resources
Tapescript of extract from start of lesson (Lawrence 1990):

Teacher reads dialogue using present continuous tense.

T: now . . . do you find any similar forms?

L: (silence)

T: well, what about chopping? . . . carrying, working . . . what do they all end in?

L: ing

T: we call that present . . . what?

L: (silence)

T: present continuous . . . when do we use present continuous?

L: (silence)

T: it is in present continuous if it is about an arrangement for the future/

   do you see? . . . so we use present continuous for a definite arrangement for the future. (T. gives examples of sentences) . . . right . . . and
   . . . I am studying at school . . . what could that be?

L: (silence)

T: what makes us use the present there?

L: (silence)

T: when somebody says this, will he use it for an action happening now
   or in the future?/

   does this describe an action happening now or in the future?

L: happening now

T: yes ... though not necessarily at this moment ... not right now because we are studying English now, not Science ... so ... we have studied three forms in which we can use present continuous tense ... that is ... (T. gives explanations again).

Procedures

1 With reference to the tapescript, analyse the way in which this teacher teaches the present continuous tense.

2 How would you describe the approach to structure teaching as prac- tised by this teacher? (See the criteria used by Lawrence in **14.4.**) You might use deductive or inductive, cognitive or mechanical, accuracy or rule-focused, etc.

3 What problems did this teacher encounter in the lesson?

4 What advice would you give to this teacher to help in overcoming these difficulties?

▶ **TASK 110**

Aim

To identify approaches to teaching structure in your teaching and learning context.

Procedures

1 Draw up an observation sheet to use when observing structure lessons. This should indicate the different approaches that teachers may use. Make sure you leave enough space on your observation sheet to write notes and to make any additions to your observation sheet.

2 Observe one class and pilot your observation sheet.

3 Arrange to observe a number of lessons where colleagues are teaching structure. You may also wish to invite a colleague to use your checklist in evaluating one of your own lessons.

4 From the data collected, are there differences in methodology accord- ing to the stage in the lesson observed, for example the presentation, practice, or production stages?

5 Encourage some of your colleagues to observe each others' classes. Try to get information from twenty or so different teachers.

6 Analyse and summarize your findings. What can you say about gram- mar teaching in your context?

7 Suggest:
   a) ways in which you could discuss your findings with other teachers;
   b) the kind of recommendations you might wish to make for the improvement of grammar teaching in your schools.

17.3 Evaluating the use of different learning activities

▶ TASK 111

Aims

To evaluate:

1 the different types of classroom activities used in classrooms by teachers in your context, for example: drills, pairwork, storytelling, songs, games;

2 the problems faced by teachers in choosing activities for a lesson;

3 the most popular activities used and why they are popular.

Procedures

1 Design an observation sheet that you could use when observing other teachers' lessons. This should record all the different types of learning activities that teachers actually use at different stages of the lesson, and the frequency with which they are used.

2 Draw up a list of questions you would ask teachers when interviewing them to find out about the problems they face when choosing activities for their lessons.

3 Decide on how you will gather this information. How many teachers? What time scale? Other issues?

4 Using your observation sheet, get teachers to observe each others' lessons and to interview each other.

5 Analyse these data and summarize the findings.

6 From your findings, which is the most popular learning activity? Did you find out why? Which is the least used? Why?

7 In what ways can you use this information formatively to develop current practice in your schools?

18   Evaluation of materials

The next tasks refer to materials evaluation. It will be useful to refer to the relevant parts in **2.4** and **9** and **10**. The first two tasks concern the evaluation of teaching and learning materials at the level of workplan.

18.1   Materials evaluation: workplan

► TASK 112

Aim
To evaluate a resource book on writing skills (Hedge 1989).

Context
You want to find some supplementary writing activities to use with a specific class.

Resource 1
On the back cover of the book you find the following description:

> *Writing* presents a range of writing tasks within a framework of current thinking on the process of writing. It discusses the components of writing ability which skilled writers demonstrate and how classroom activities can help learners to develop these. The first part of the book focuses on 'authoring' skills: developing a sense of audience, planning, drafting, and revising. The second section considers elements of 'crafting': the way in which a writer puts together the pieces of the text and chooses correct and appropriate language. The tasks are designed in relation to a variety of writing purposes and a range of text types for general purpose language learners.

(Hedge 1989)

Procedure

1 Read the description with a view to making an initial decision about whether to buy the book and use it as a reference book.

2 What other information do you think you need about the book?

Resource 2

Here are some extracts from the Table of Contents of *Writing*:

1 Composing			19
Activity	*Level*	*Topic*	
1.1 Gathering information	Lower intermediate	My earliest years	26
1.2 Pyramid planning	Lower intermediate upwards	First day at school	28
1.3 Making mind maps	Intermediate to advanced	A festival	30
2 Communicating			61
2.1 Exchanging letters with your students	Elementary to advanced	Personal topics	65
2.2 Sharing journals with students	Elementary to advanced	Any personal or learning topic	66
2.3 Getting to know your group	Elementary to advanced	Our group or our class	67
3 Crafting			89
3.1 Organizing a non-chronological description	Intermediate	A scene as a moment in time	101
3.2 Using connectors of addition	Lower intermediate upwards	Leisure activities	103
3.3 Using cohesive devices	Intermediate	A school guide	105
3.4 Analysing the reference system of a text	Intermediate	The Eskimos	107
3.5 Organizing general and supporting statements	Advanced	Stress	109
4 Improving			145
4.1 Designing a grading scheme	Intermediate to advanced	Marking compositions	153
4.2 Conferencing	Intermediate	A review	154
4.3 Raising awareness about writing	Intermediate to advanced	A questionnaire on writing	155

(Hedge 1989)

Procedure

1 After reading the Table of Contents, what useful additional information do you now have?

2 Can you now make the decision to buy the book? Do you need more information?

Resource 3

The following is an extract from one of the exercises in the section on 'composing':

COMPOSING

LEVEL	**Lower intermediate upwards**
TOPIC	**Surveying social issues**
PREPARATION	During the task it is useful if you can make copies of questionnaires which the students produce. Alternatively, each student could be asked to make several handwritten copies.
IN CLASS	1 Tell the students that they are going to work in groups to make a questionnaire on a subject of their own choice or one suggested by you.
	2 Choose an example to discuss with the class. Use it to elicit and discuss the kind of information they want to obtain and what questions they would ask. For example, with the topic 'Banning cyclists from the road', students might consider a first question:
	– *Are you a cyclist or a driver or both?*
	or
	– *Do you think of yourself mostly as a driver or a cyclist?*
	Further questions can then be directed at each category, e.g. to cyclists:
	– *How often do you cycle?*
	– *Where do you cycle?*
	– *What are the main dangers for cyclists?*
	– *Is there good provision for cyclists?*
	– *What do you think of drivers?*
	3 The students decide on a topic in their groups, write out their questionnaire and check it with you. Your role at this stage is to monitor the group work, give advice, and prompt.
	4 Groups can then carry out a survey using their questionnaires. If they are in language schools in an English-speaking environment, students can interview host families, local contacts, and people in the street. In non-English-speaking situations, they can interview members of their own class and other classes.
FOLLOW-UP	In a follow-up session, groups discuss the information they have managed to collect and write a report of their results, with conclusions. This could be preceded by a presentation from you of the kind of language needed:

– *Almost everybody*	*reported that . . .*
– *The majority of people*	*said that . . .*
– *A minority of people*	*thought that*
– *Only a few people*	*complained that . . .*

(Hedge 1989:57)

Procedures

1 Using all three pieces of information (Resources 1, 2, and 3), make an evaluative decision about the usefulness of buying the book for your teaching situation.

2 Would you buy the book for your personal use or would it be more suitable for the English Department's resources library?

► **TASK 113**

Aim
To evaluate the suitability of a textbook for use in an EFL classroom.

Resource 1
The Course Outline from an intermediate level coursebook (Black et al., *Fast Forward 2 Classbook*, 1987) follows:

SCOPE AND SEQUENCE CHART

Page	Unit	Communicative Functions	Topics and Vocabulary	Language Focus
2	Introductory Unit	Introductions	Getting to know each other Leisure Work	Present Simple Question forms Relative clauses: who Gerund/Infinitive
7	1	Asking for and giving directions Asking for information Saying where places are Describing places	Edinburgh Tourist information Towns	Prepositions
11	2	Offers and requests Arrangements Suggestions Hopes and plans	Food and drink Business conferences Entertainment	Modals: could/would/can Present Continuous for future arrangements Degrees of certainty
16	3	Complaining Apologizing Offering to put things right Accepting or refusing offers	Consumer problems Shopping	Present Perfect
20	**Review Unit 1** Part 1	Revision	Multicultural Britain Eating out in Britain Unemployment	Revision
	Part 2	Project	Finding out about other countries	
26	4	Describing things Describing people	Natural things Personality	Word order Relative clauses
31	5	Comparison Describing processes	Statistics Developing world Chewing gum	Passives Sequencing

36	6	Describing past actions and events	Customs and beliefs Myths	Past tenses Sequencing
40	**Review Unit 2** Part 1	Revision	Britain: people, places and accents	Revision
	Part 2	Simulation	Dalelakemoor	
46	7	Asking for and giving advice	Advice agencies Protecting your home 'Neighbourhood Watch'	Modals: should/ought to Gerund
51	8	Asking for and giving opinions Agreeing and disagreeing Expressing no opinion	Modern life Issues and causes	Link words Neither/Either
55	9	Expressing feelings Reacting	Gestures Romantic fiction	Adjective formation: ing/ed Question tags
61	**Review Unit 3** Part 1	Revision	The British education system The Open University	Revision
	Part 2	Simulation	Kelapia	
70	10	Expressing certainty and uncertainty Speculating about the future	Science fiction	1st and 2nd Conditionals
76	11	Deducing Speculating	Museum pieces Mysteries: The Bermuda Triangle	Modals: can/can't/may could/couldn't/ must/might
81	12	Regretting Wishing and hoping	A chapter of accidents Martin Luther King	3rd Conditional
86	**Review Unit 4** Part 1	Revision	Ethnic groups in Britain Carnivals and festivals	Revision
	Part 2	Course review	Ways out and on	

(Black et al. 1987:iv)

Procedures

1 Assume you have to choose a coursebook for a group of intermediate learners.

a) Write out your own requirements for a coursebook (see **2.4, 9,** and **10** on materials evaluation).

b) Make a list of the criteria that are important to you when evaluating materials for possible use in your context.

2 Read the Course Outline given above and make an initial decision about the suitability of this book for a group of intermediate learners you know. What conclusions have you drawn so far?

Resource 2

Extracts from the Introduction to the Teacher's Book (Black et al., *Fast Forward 2*, 1988b) follow:

Who is this course for?

Fast Forward 2 is designed for intermediate students who are interested in approaching the English language in a stimulating and interesting way. It is not suitable for anyone who believes that learning involves suffering. The authors have sought to bring pleasure and challenge to the learning process whilst keeping their materials based firmly on sound communicative principles. The course will be found particularly appropriate for learners on short intensive courses, where these materials were originally developed, but can be used to good effect with any group of committed adult learners.

What view of language underlies the course?

A look at the Lesson Plans at the beginning of each unit and the Scope and Sequence chart at the end of this introduction will reveal not just that the materials are communicatively based, but also that full account has been taken of all factors which contribute to successful communication: a confident command of structure, a good working vocabulary, sensitivity to the differing types of language appropriate in various situations, familiarity with a wide range of text types, a good balance between the skills of listening, reading, speaking and writing. There is also an implicit admission that language is complex: there is no attempt to delude the learners with over-simplification or to 'baby' them with graded down material. Instead, the authors have elected to organize the course into units, each containing a manageable 'chunk' of new language to focus on. In particular, the materials reflect a clear awareness that adult learners bring a certain degree of linguistic experience to the learning of English, and that this experience can be used to good advantage.

What methodological principles underlie the course?

The keynote here is flexibility. In the firm belief that the 'How?' of teaching will differ according to circumstances, the authors have offered a 'learning package' which can be regarded more as a teaching resource than just a textbook.

It is perfectly possible to use the book as a traditional course, beginning at the beginning and working through to the end; indeed, many learners and teachers may be happy with such an approach, for the present order of the units and of the activities in each unit is the most obvious one, and arises from the authors' own classroom experience. It may, however, be equally valid, with a particular group, to start at another point in the book, and to base the teaching programme on learners' linguistic needs or thematic interests.

How are the learners' needs met in the course?

In this course, the authors aim to keep faith with the learner by providing, in addition to the Classbook, a Resource Book containing summaries of essential language points as well as extra practice exercises for learners to tackle out of class. In recognition of a need for grammatical and lexical consolidation in a course with a communicative basis, many of these exercises focus on structures or vocabulary development.

The inclusion of the Tapescript and Answer Key means that the students can, if they prefer, work on their own. As a further aid to learning, a review unit has been built into the Classbook every after three learning units to enable both learners and teacher to take stock of progress and to revise. By reference to these units learners will be able to see and measure their own progress, and will not have to rely solely on the teacher's judgement.

Finally there is an implicit recognition that not all learners move forward at the same pace, and that some are stronger in certain skills than others. The Resource Book contains exercises which can be used as extra material for faster learners and this Teacher's Book contains suggestions for further activity, as well as photocopiable extra material.

A glance at the range of exercises and activities in each unit will reveal a balance between 'closed' and 'open' tasks, and between traditional exercises and more innovative activities. This represents an acknowledgement that different learners learn in different ways and find different activities useful. The aim is to provide something for everyone: thus the convergent thinker will probably prefer the 'closed' type of task, whilst the divergent thinker will find more to challenge her or him in open-ended activities.

How does all this affect me as a teacher?

The flexibility and variety that has been built into the course means that the teacher will have to be adaptable in her/his own approach. There will be times when she/he will prefer to keep a low profile as learners work on a fluency exercise in groups or pairs; at other times there is a need for a more teacher-controlled approach. The more experienced teacher will make comparatively little reference to the teacher's notes; they are written to make course and lesson planning easier for her/his less experienced counterpart.

What does a unit contain?

The only really common factor is that each unit offers material for 1½–2 hours of classwork. The variety of approach mentioned above means that each unit is different from the last one.

New language points are presented in each unit, but in different ways. Sometimes a text is used, sometimes a dialogue, sometimes the emphasis is on visuals, sometimes on a communicative task.

Each unit offers a balance of exercise and activity types to appeal to the different kinds of learner mentioned above. One learner may prefer a test plus exercises type of approach as it is fairly familiar: another may be happy to be stimulated to produce new language directly at the start of a unit.

There are a wide variety of listening passages including some which are authentic or adapted authentic and will therefore prove challenging. It may be advisable for the students to look at the exercises first, before listening, to provide clues as to what to listen for. Providing students with a copy of the tapescript may also be necessary for some groups. Emphasize however that the important point is always to understand the information relevant to the task and not every word. Exposure to authentic listening is important as early as possible to allow students to 'panic' in the safety of the classroom and therefore be better prepared for real life situations.

Procedures

1 Using resources 1 and 2 above, to what extent do you think that this textbook will or will not be useful to you for your specified purposes? Why?

2 What other needs have you got? What further information would still be useful to you?

3 What other procedures would you use to complete your evaluation?

18.2 Materials evaluation: classroom use

For the next materials evaluation tasks, we invite you to think abut the ways that you would evaluate a set of supplementary reading materials in use. In other words, we would like you to suggest ways in which materials may be evaluated while they are being used with groups of learners in the classroom.

▶ TASK 114

Aim

To evaluate the use of learning materials in one of your classes.

Procedures

1 Record one of your classes or observe a class of one of your colleagues.

2 Select a unit from one of your coursebooks, a set of learning activities, or another kind of material you wish to evaluate.

3 Make a list of questions, the answers to which will give you an indication of how the materials are actually being used with effect in class. Five questions are given as a guide:
   a) What objectives should be achieved through using these materials?
   b) How do you expect the teacher to use the materials?
   c) How do you expect the learners to use and react to the materials?
   d) Do you think the materials are at the appropriate level for the learners? If not, what recommendations would you make to modify them?
   e) How many learners reacted positively to the materials? How many seemed uninterested in them?
   Make additions to this list.

4 Analyse, with reference to the questions you have asked, how these materials actually worked in the class with the learners. To what extent do you think the materials worked well? Why? To what extent do you think the materials were limited? Why? Which of these limitations did you predict? Which were those that you did not predict? What modifications to the materials would you suggest for future use with another similar class?

▶ TASK 115

Aim

To evaluate the different ways of evaluating materials.

Resources

The data from the Tasks in **18** (Tasks 111 to 113).

Procedures

1 Consider Tasks 112 to 114 and these two approaches to evaluating teaching and learning materials: (1) before using them in the classroom, i.e. at the level of workplan; (2) while they are in actual classroom use.

2 Which stage do you think provides the most information about the worth of the materials? Why?

3 What are the notable differences in the two evaluations? Give the advantages and disadvantages.

19 Teacher evaluation

The next tasks relate to teacher evaluation; we invite you to focus primarily on evaluation for purposes of teacher self-development. It is at this level that evaluations provide rich data. It is also at this level that successful implementation of curriculum innovations to a large extent depends, in terms of acceptance, on the resourcefulness of teachers.

19.1 Motivating learners

▶ **TASK 116**

Aim
To investigate the ways in which you and other teaching colleagues motivate your learners.

Procedures
1 There are several ways in which teachers motivate or demotivate their learners. Consider the following:
   – using praising words or gestures;
   – encouraging only a small number of learners to contribute to the lesson;
   – setting realistic learning goals;
   – ignoring a learner's contribution;
   – providing the learners with a challenge;
   – providing the opportunity for meaningful communication to take place;
   – giving learners responsibilities in a task;
   – providing interesting topics to work on.
   Make additions to this list.

2 Design an observation checklist that reflects ways in which a teacher might motivate learners.

3 Prepare a questionnaire for:
   a) teachers, about how they feel they motivate learners;
   b) learners, about how they feel teachers try to motivate them in class.

4 Arrange to observe a lesson or make a recording of a lesson. Use one of your own or that of a colleague.

5 Use the checklist to analyse the lesson you observe or the recording you have made. Make a note of each time a particular item is observed.

6 Evaluate your results. You might find it useful to reflect on whether the teacher's action (either yours or that of a colleague) resulted in a greater degree of motivation in the learners or the opposite.

19.2 Teacher leadership styles

▶ TASK 117

Aim
To evaluate the dominant style of teacher leadership in the class.

Procedures
1 Record one of your own classes or observe a class of one of your colleagues.

2 Design a checklist or an observation schedule (see **1.4** and **3.3**).
Consider the following entries for your observation checklist:
  – the degree of control by the teacher
  – the amount of controlled practice compared with free practice
  – teacher-fronted activities
  – learner-centred activities
  – the kind of instructions given to learners
  – the teacher's tone, for example soft spoken or loud.
  – the way learners are disciplined
  – the bearing of the teacher, for example authoritative or approachable
  – the degree of freedom for learners to negotiate the course and content of the lesson
  – does the teacher impose decisions?
  – classroom arrangement: whose decision? what does it show?

3 Using your checklist analyse the recording or the observation in order to outline the main features of your (or your colleague's) style during different parts of the lesson; for your discussion of the overall style you might include autocratic and controlling (tells), paternalist and persuading (sells), consultative and negotiating (involves), democratic and participating (planning together on equal terms as described in Everard and Morris 1990), or combinations, for example mostly paternalist but sometimes consultative.

4 Suggest ways in which you might use the findings as a basis for change (your behaviour or that of your colleague's) in the classroom, for example adopting appropriate styles for different parts of the lesson, such as less controlling in the free practice or group work.

▶ **TASK 118**

Aim

To evaluate the kinds of support a teacher may give to learners in the classroom.

Procedures

1 Record your own class or observe that of a colleague.

2 Design a checklist for your observation or recording analysis. An observation schedule might include the following points: obvious support (praise), indirect support, rewarding, punishing, challenging, empathy, emotional support, listening, structuring tasks, shouting, encouraging, motivating speech and gestures, individual attention.

3 Evaluate your data using the observation schedule.

4 Compare the kinds of support given and decide on a general description of the support given by you or your colleague.

5 Suggest ways in which you might want to vary the type of support you or your colleague might give in the classroom, corresponding to the situation, at different stages in the lesson or the time of the year such as approaching examinations.

19.3 Question types

▶ **TASK 119**

Aim

To analyse the kinds of questions used by teachers in the classroom.

Procedures

1 Record your own lesson or with the cooperation of a colleague, observe a class.

2 Using the observation sheet made in **16.4**, make an analysis of either the recording or the lesson.

3 Discuss the overall outcome of the observation data with your colleague.

4 What overall picture are you getting about the style of classroom interaction, for example, learner- or teacher-centred? What evidence can you give for your opinion?

5 What steps would you like to take as a result of your enquiry to make future lessons more learner-centred (for example using more open-ended questions)?

6 Choose another later occasion to record and observe a class in order to compare the findings and note any changes in approach.

19.4 Homework: setting, marking, and giving feedback

▶ TASK 120

Aim

To evaluate the pattern of setting homework, for example the type of homework set and frequency.

Context

You want to find out about the kind of homework teachers in your situation set. You may want to include items such as written homework, making notes for an oral presentation, reading preparation, working on a part of a class project, or learning vocabulary items.

Procedures

1 Design an appropriate procedure for teachers to find out about the kind and frequency of homework they set. For example, you may wish to use a questionnaire (see **16.2** and **16.3**) or an interview (see **16.5**).

2 Prepare a questionnaire for learners so that they can be asked for similar information.

3 Collect your data.

4 Summarize your findings.

5 Explain why you think certain types of homework are popular with teachers.

6 You may wish to interview a couple of teachers to ask them why they prefer the most popular types of homework set.

7 Monitor homework setting in a number of classes over a period of time, say six classes in one week.

8 Now compare all the results that you have: from the teachers, from the learners, and from your survey of homework set in any one week. Is there a consensus view?

9 Make a list of the things that you could now do to bring about improvements in the setting of homework based on your small survey.

▶ TASK 121

Aim

To evaluate the kinds of feedback given to learners after they have been set homework.

Procedures

1 Select a class and collect a sample of written homework that has been returned to learners.

2 Record or observe a teacher's comments as homework is returned in class or, in the case of learner feedback in small groups, of a small group of learners who are exchanging comments on their work.

3 Examine the scripts for comments about the homework. Look out for how the teacher annotates the work: percentage marks, grades, or symbols such as gr=grammar error or sp=spelling mistake.

4 Note the frequency of each type of marking scheme.

5 From the recording or from your observation, summarize the type of comments made (by both teachers and learners) and the action that follows these comments. For this you may find it useful to prepare an observation sheet based on the design of those described in **3.3**, especially Arrowsmith 1989.

6 Summarize the findings from your evaluation.

7 Make recommendations on the ways that you would like to follow up your findings with a group of teachers in your own school.

▶ TASK 122

Aim
To evaluate the effectiveness of feedback on homework to learners.

Procedures
1 Write a questionnaire asking learners how they think homework is useful and what they have learned from the feedback they receive on their homework tasks. You might help them to focus on some specific items they learned in a week or in a unit of work.

2 Prepare a second questionnaire to administer to class teachers on their attitudes towards the usefulness of feedback on homework.

3 Compare the answers you receive from learners and from teachers. Describe the similarities and differences.

4 What conclusions could you draw? What action would you like to take as a result of your evaluation?

19.5 Teacher self-evaluation

▶ TASK 123

Aim
To self-evaluate a particular aspect of your own teaching which you would like to improve or that you find problematic. (see **3.4** and 'Teacher self-evaluation' in **2.5**).

Procedures

1 Choose a particular aspect of your teaching you want to investigate and plan a lesson to highlight this aspect, for example, the teaching of grammar.

2 Discuss with a colleague:
   a) how and when the evaluation could be carried out;
   b) the areas you wish to be observed, for example presentation of grammar items.

3 Draw up an observation schedule with your colleague. This might include:
   beginning the presentation, illustrating the grammar item, lead into controlled practice, monitoring the controlled practice, the effectiveness of the free practice exercise, responses to learner questions or requests for clarification etc.

4 a) Undertake the observation in one class (over a period of time)
   b) Record and analyse the lesson.

5 Discuss and analyse the findings with your colleagues.

6 Decide what action will you take, for example diagrams and tables to illustrate clearly the grammar item.

20 Evaluating learner outcomes

▶ TASK 124

Aim
To evaluate different approaches to evaluation of learner performance.

Resource 1
Here is a self-assessment form adapted from Oskarsson (quoted in Lewkowicz and Moon 1985:54–5)

Instructions: Put a cross (x) in the box which you think best indicates your ability to complete the task below.

Imagine that someone with no knowledge of English comes to you with an English daily newspaper and asks you to give a detailed account of what is on the front page. You have plenty of time, but must not use a dictionary.

I would be able to give a detailed account of everything on the front page. ⟶ 5 ☐

4 ☐

3 ☐

2 ☐

1 ☐

I would not be able to say anything. ⟶ 0 ☐

(Continues overleaf)

Instructions: Put a cross (x) in the box which you think best describes your reading ability.

I read and understand the language as well as a well-educated native.	5	☐
	4.5	☐
I understand everything or nearly everything written in the language within non-specialized fields. There may be words I do not understand in difficult texts.	4	☐
	3.5	☐
I understand most of what I read in simple texts dealing with familiar subjects such as leisure interests, current affairs and living conditions. I understand most of a normal private letter dealing with everyday things such as the family and their activities. I understand the main contents of a normal newspaper article about a plane crash or the opening of a new underground line, for example, but not all the details	3	☐
	2.5	☐
I understand the meaning of simple written instructions about the way, time, place and similar things, and also understand the essential things in simple texts dealing with familiar subjects such as common leisure interests, current affairs and living conditions.	2	☐
	1.5	☐
I understand the main points of a simple text and simple written directions for familiar things.	1	☐
	0.5	☐
I cannot read the language at all.	0	☐

(Oskarsson 1978)

Resource 2
Here is an example of recorded observations from *Patterns of Learning*:

Date	Reading
	Record observations of the child's development as a reader (including wider experiences of story) across a range of contexts
Oct. 88	Reading for information: T. can identify sections of text which provide info. he needs – he's just worked out strategies for doing this, e.g. using contents list/index, then looking for relevant information.
Feb. 89	Keen to take part in discussions about how a story unfolds in a plot – takes the lead in discussions and takes work seriously.
June 89	Only comprehends nuances of text/literary allusions e.g. puns with help, but takes them on board quickly when explained.

(Barrs et al. 1990:21)

Procedures
1 In which ways are these two approaches to evaluating a learner's language abilities the same and different from those you use when evaluating learners?
2 In which ways are these examples similar and different?
3 To what extent are 'tests' like these useful to
   a) teachers?
   b) learners?

▶ TASK 125
Aim
To evaluate teacher reactions to the use of profiling as a means of evaluating learners.

Resource
Look at the extract on page 45 and the examples in **13.3** (from the Primary Language Record).

Procedures

1 On your own, or with a colleague, write out questions for a question-naire designed to get reactions from your colleagues about the use of profiling in their classrooms.

2 Administer the questionnaire.

3 Interview one or two teachers as a follow-up to their answers to the questionnaire.

4 Analyse and summarize your findings.

5 Make a list of the positive finding from your evaluation.

6 Make a list of the negative findings from your evaluation.

7 Overall, in what ways could profiling be a useful supplement to the ways in which teachers can evaluate learners?

8 What are the implications of your evaluation for future action?

Glossary

accountability: used in this volume in the sense of having to give account of what has been done (often in a project) in terms of 'value for money' and overall impact.

communicative: refers in this volume to an approach to teaching languages which emphasizes the importance of language use and communication, and which uses a range of learning activities as a means to this end.

contingency: used in the sense of a style of management which characterizes the teaching and learning context in terms of task, group, and individual needs.

deductive: an approach to teaching grammar which explicitly explains and demonstrates a grammatical rule before practical activities are introduced.

formative: this refers to evaluation activities—as an ongoing process—that are undertaken at regular intervals with a view to using the evaluation 'results' as a basis for future action.

inductive: an approach to teaching grammar which allows the learner to infer/absorb grammatical rules through practice and use.

innovation: something new that arises from a planned (as opposed to an unplanned) change in relation to an aspect of the teaching/learning curriculum.

observation schedule: a checklist or table containing items to be observed during a lesson(s); it provides space to record details of the observations (e.g. frequency, sequence) and, possibly, additional comments.

evaluation procedures: techniques used to obtain evaluation data when carrying out an evaluation; questionnaires, observation schedules, and interviews are examples of evaluation procedures.

profile: documents the achievement of learners in descriptive terms.

structural: an approach to language teaching which focuses on grammatical structures and systems.

summative: an evaluation undertaken at the end or a project, programme, of course.

synthetic: an approach to grammar teaching which deals with discrete items of grammar out of context.

Further reading

Procedures for evaluating classrooms
Three books provide useful and accessible accounts of different ways of investigating the language classroom:

Hopkins, D. 1985. *A Teacher's Guide to Classroom Research*. Milton Keynes: Open University Press.

Nunan, D. 1989. *Understanding Language Classrooms*. London: Prentice Hall International.

van Lier, L. 1988. *The Classroom and the Language Learner*. London: Longman.

On management/innovation

Robbins, S. 1989. *Training in Interpersonal Skills*. London: Prentice Hall International.
A practical guide providing tips for those involved in management or management training. Includes some good awareness-raising questionnaires followed by discussion of management principles and some role-play activities.

Rudduck, J. 1991. *Innovation and Change*. Milton Keynes: Open University Press.
An account and reflection on the practical difficulties of introducing educational innovation in Britain. Serious consideration is given to learner involvement.

On developmental aspects of evaluation
This is usefully analysed in:

Hopkins, D. 1989. *Evaluation for School Development*. Milton Keynes: Open University Press.

On Testing

Heaton, J. B. 1990. *Classroom Testing*. London: Longman.
This offers a concise and non-technical account of classroom testing and provides useful examples for its readers.

Notes on examinations

The International English Language Testing System (IELTS) supersedes the earlier English Language Testing Service (ELTS). IELTS is a language proficiency test for non-native speakers of English who intend to study or train through the medium of English. IELTS is jointly managed by the British Council, the University of Cambridge Local Examinations Syndicate (UCLES), and the International Development Program of Australian Universities and Colleges (IDP) and is administered by UCLES.

For further information please contact:

IELTS Subject Officer, UCLES, 1 Hills Road, Cambridge, CB1 2EU, UK

or:

The Manager, IELTS (Australia), GPO Box 2006, Canberra, ACT 2601, Australia

The Diploma in Teaching English as a Foreign Language was formerly administered by the Royal Society of Arts, but is now administered under the joint name of RSA/UCLES.

The Test of English as a Foreign Language (TOEFL) is administered by the Educational Testing Service (ETS), Princeton, New Jersey, USA. It is a proficiency test intended for students wishing to study through the medium of English in American universities. It is also recognized in many institutions in other English-speaking countries.

Bibliography

Alderson, J. C. 1985. *Evaluation*. Lancaster Practical Papers in English Language Education 6. Oxford: Pergamon.

Allen, P., and S. Carroll. 1987. 'Evaluation of classroom processes in a Canadian core French programme.' *Evaluation and Research in Education* 1/2:49–61.

Allen, P., M. Fröhlich, and N. Spada. 1983. 'The communicative orientation of language teaching: an observation scheme.' In: J. Handscome, R. A. Orem, and B. P. Taylor (eds.): *On TESOL:83. The Question of Control*. Washington, DC:TESOL, 1983.

Allwright, D. 1975. 'Problems in the study of teachers' treatment of learner error.' In: M. K. Burt and H. C. Dulay (eds.): *On Tesol:75. New directions in second language learning, teaching, and bilingual education*. Washington, DC:TESOL, 1975.

Allwright, D. 1981. 'What do we need materials for?' *English Language Teaching Journal* 36/1:6–9.

Arrowsmith, R. 1988. 'Teacher feedback to oral errors.' Unpublished assignment. London: Ealing College London (now Polytechnic of West London).

Barrs, M., S. Ellis, H. Hester, and A. Thomas. 1988. *The Primary Language Record: Handbook for Teachers*. London: ILEA/Centre for Language in Primary Education (Webber Row, London SE1 8QW).

Barrs, M., S. Ellis, H. Hester, and A. Thomas. 1990. *Patterns of Learning*. London: Centre for Language in Primary Education (Webber Row, London SE1 8QW).

Beretta, A. and A. Davies. 1985. 'Evaluation of the Bangalore Project.' *English Language Teaching Journal* 39/2:121–7.

Black, V., M. McNorton, A. Malderez, and S. Parker. 1987. *Fast Forward 2: Classbook*. Oxford: Oxford University Press.

Black, V., M. McNorton, A. Malderez, and S. Parker. 1988a. *Fast Forward 2: Resource Book*. Oxford: Oxford University Press.

Black, V., M. McNorton, A. Malderez, and S. Parker. 1988b. *Fast Forward 2: Teacher's Book*. Oxford: Oxford University Press.

Bolitho, R. and G. James (eds.) *Teacher Assessment: Report of the 1982 Exeter Seminar*. Exeter: Language Centre, University of Exeter.

Breen, M. 1989. 'The evaluation cycle for language learning tasks.' In: R. K. Johnson (ed.): *The Second Language Curriculum*. Cambridge: Cambridge University Press, 1989.

Breen, M. P. and **C. N. Candlin.** 1987. 'Which materials?: a consumer's and designer's guide.' In: L. E. Sheldon (ed.): *ELT Textbooks and Materials: Problems in Evaluation and Development*. ELT Documents. London: Modern English Publications/British Council, 1987.

Brindley, G. 1989. *Assessing Achievement in the Learner-Centred Curriculum*. Sydney: National Centre for English Language Teaching and Research.

Brumfit, C. 1984. *Communicative Methodology in Language Teaching*. Cambridge: Cambridge University Press.

Bryman, A. 1986. *Leadership and Organisations*. London: Routledge and Kegan Paul.

Chaudron, C. 1977. 'A descriptive model of discourse in the corrective treatment of learners' errors.' In *Language Learning* 27/1:29–49.

Clarke, J. L. D. 1969. 'The Pennsylvania Project and the "Audiolingual vs. Traditional" question.' *Modern Language Journal* 53:388–96.

Cole, G. A. 1983. *Management Theory and Practice*. Eastleigh, Hants: D. P. Publications Ltd.

Cunningsworth, A. 1984. *Evaluating and Selecting EFL Teaching Materials*. London: Heinemann.

Cunningsworth, A. 1987. *Coursebooks and Conversational Skills*. ELT Documents. London: Modern English Publications/British Council.

Dunkin, M. and **J. Biddle.** 1974. *The Study of Teaching*. New York: Holt, Reinhart, and Winston.

Ellis, R. (ed.) 1989. 'Monitoring and administration of a test in teacher training materials for testing.' Unpublished mimeograph. London: Ealing College London (now Polytechnic of West London).

Ellis, R. and **M. Rathbone.** 1987. *The Acquisition of German in a Classroom Context*. London: Ealing College London (now Polytechnic of West London).

Everard, K. B. 1986. *Developing Management In Schools*. Oxford: Blackwell.

Everard, K. B. and **G. Morris.** 1990. *Effective School Management*. London: Paul Chapman Publishing.

Examinations in English as a Foreign Language: Certificates and Diplomas for Language Teachers (examiners' handbook). 1988. Cambridge: RSA/UCLES.

Fröhlich, M., N. Spada, and **P. Allen.** 1985. 'Differences in the communicative orientation of L2 classrooms.' *TESOL Quarterly* 19/1:27–57.

Germaine, K. P. 1989. 'An investigation of leadership traits and skills in relation to microteaching feedback sessions in ELT teacher education.' Unpublished MA dissertation. London: Ealing College London (now Polytechnic of West London).

Greenwood, J. 1985. 'Bangalore revisited: a reluctant complaint.' *English Language Teaching Journal* 39/4:268–73.

Hedge, T. 1989. *Writing*. Oxford: Oxford University Press.

Hopkins, D. 1985. *A Teacher's Guide to Classroom Research*. Milton Keynes: Open University Press.

An Introduction to IELTS. 1989. Cambridge: UCLES/British Council; Canberra, Australia: International Development Program of Australian Universities and Colleges.

James, G. 1983. *Teacher Assessment 2: Report of the Second Exeter Seminar.* Exeter: Language Centre, University of Exeter.

Kemmis, S. and R. McTaggart. 1982. *The Action Research Planner.* Victoria, Australia: Deakin University Press.

Kouraogo, P. 1987. 'Curriculum renewal and INSET in difficult circumstances.' *English Language Teaching Journal* 41/3:171–8.

Krashen, S. and T. Terrell. 1983. *The Natural Method: Language Acquisition in the Classroom.* Oxford: Pergamon.

Lawrence, L. 1990. 'Language in Education: An evaluation of the teaching of structure in Zambian grade 8 classes.' Unpublished PhD thesis. Lusaka: University of Zambia.

Lewkowicz, J. A. and J. Moon. 1985. 'Evaluation: a way of involving the learner.' In J. C. Alderson (ed.): *Evaluation.* Lancaster Practical Papers in English Language Education 6. Oxford: Pergamon, 1985.

Low, G. 1987. 'The need for a multi-perspective approach to the evaluation of foreign language teaching materials.' *Evaluation and Research in Education* 1/1.

Malamah-Thomas, A. 1987. *Classroom Interaction.* Oxford: Oxford University Press.

McNiff, J. 1988. *Action Research: Principles and Practice.* Basingstoke: Macmillan Educational.

Miletto, H. 1989. 'Error analysis.' Unpublished assignment. London: Ealing College London (now Polytechnic of West London).

Miletto, H. 1990. ' "Self evaluation form", Young workers' and youth leaders' course.' Unpublished assignment. London: Ealing College London (now Polytechnic of West London).

Mitchell, R., B. Parkinson, and R. Johnstone. 1981. *The Foreign Language Classroom: An Observational Study.* Stirling, Scotland: Department of Education, University of Stirling.

Moore, J. 1980. 'Materials development: a case study.' In: *English for Specific Purposes: An International Seminar.* 17–22 April 1977. London: British Council.

Moyles, J. 1988. *Self-evaluation: A Primary Teacher's Guide.* Windsor: NFER-Nelson.

Murphy-O'Dwyer, L. 1985. 'Diary studies as a method for evaluating teacher training.' In: J. C. Alderson (ed.): *Evaluation.* Lancaster Practical Papers in English Language Education 6. Oxford: Pergamon, 1985.

Nisbet, J. 1987. 'The role of evaluation in accountability systems.' In: R. Murphy and H. Torrance (eds.): *Evaluating Education: Issues and Methods.* London: Harper and Row, 1987.

Nunan, D. 1988. *The Learner-centred Curriculum.* Cambridge: Cambridge University Press.

Nunan, D. 1989. *Understanding Language Classrooms.* New York: Prentice Hall International.

O'Dell, F. 1990. 'A useful clarifier.' *EFL Gazette* 122:22.

Oskarsson, M. 1978. *Approaches to Self-assessment in Foreign Language Learning*. Oxford: Pergamon Press.

Parlett, M. and D. Hamilton. 1987. 'Evaluation as illumination: a new approach to the study of innovatory programmes.' In: R. Murphy and H. Torrance (eds.): *Evaluating Education: Issues and Methods*. London: Harper and Row, 1987.

Prabhu, N. S. 1982. *The Communicational Teaching Project*. London: British Council.

Prabhu, N. S. 1987. *Second Language Pedagogy*. Oxford: Oxford University Press.

Rea-Dickins, P. M. 1989. 'Decisions about testing for language teaching purposes.' Keynote address, Japanese Association of Language Teachers (JALT). University of Tsukuba, Japan.

Rowntree, D. 1977 *Assessing Students: How Shall We Know Them?* New York: Harper and Row.

Scherer, G. A. C. and M. Wertheimer. 1964. *A Psycho-linguistic Experiment in Foreign Language Teaching*. New York: McGraw-Hill.

Sheldon, L. E. (ed.) 1987. *ELT Textbooks and Materials: Problems in Evaluation and Development*. ELT Documents. London: Modern English Publications/British Council.

Sinclair, J. McH. and R. M. Coulthard. 1975. *Towards an Analysis of Discourse*. Oxford: Oxford University Press.

Spada, N. 1987. 'Relationships between instructional differences and learning outcomes: A process-product study of communicative language teaching.' *Applied Linguistics* 8/2:142.

Stenhouse, L. 1975. *An Introduction to Curriculum Research and Development*. London: Heinemann Educational.

Stenhouse, L. 1980. *Curriculum Research and Development in Action*. London: Heinemann Educational.

Stenhouse, L. 1988 (revised edition). *An Introduction to Curriculum Research and Development*. London: Heinemann Educational.

Swan, M. 1980. *Practical English Usage*. Oxford: Oxford University Press.

West, R. 1987. *A Consumer's Guide to ELT Dictionaries*. ELT Documents. London: Modern English Publications/British Council.

Widdowson, H. G. 1978. *Teaching Language as Communication*. Oxford: Oxford University Press.

Williams, D. 1983. 'Developing criteria for textbook evaluation.' *English Language Teaching Journal* 37/3:255.

Williams, M. 1989. 'A developmental view of classroom observations.' *English Language Teaching Journal* 43/2:85–91.

Wilkins, D. 1976. *Notional Syllabuses*. Oxford: Oxford University Press.

Index

Entries relate to Sections One, Two, and Three of the text, and to the glossary. References to the glossary are indicated by 'g'.

Acknowledgements

The publishers and authors would like to thank the following for their kind permission to use articles, extracts, or adaptations from copyright material. There are instances where we have been unable to trace or contact the copyright holder before our printing deadline. We apologize for this apparent negligence. If notified the publisher will be pleased to rectify any errors or omissions at the earliest opportunity.

R. Arrowsmith, J. Linghai, A. Jurado-Spruch, and H. Miletto for the use of material from 'Error Analysis', an unpublished assignment while at Ealing College (now Polytechnic of West London).

Basil Blackwell Publishers for an extract from *Developing Management in Schools* (1986) by K. B. Everard.

V. Black, M. McNorton, A. Malderez, and S. Parker for extracts from *Fast Forward 2: Resource Book* (1988), *Classbook* (1987), and *Teachers' Book* (1988).

The British Council for extracts from: 'Materials Development: A case study' by J. Moore (1980), in *English for Specific Purposes: An International Seminar* held in Bogota, 17–22 April 1977 and *The Communicational Teaching Project* by N. S. Prabhu (1982). The British Council and Modern English Publications for extracts from *A Consumer's Guide to ELT Dictionaries* (1987) by R. West, ELT Documents, and 'Which materials? A consumers' and designers' guide' by M. P. Breen and C. N. Candlin, in L. E. Sheldon (ed.): *ELT Textbooks and Materials: Problems in Evaluation and Development* (1987), ELT Documents.

Cambridge University Press for an extract from 'The evaluation cycle for language tasks' by M. P. Breen, in R. K. Johnson (ed.): *The Second Language Curriculum* (1989).

The Centre for Language in Primary Education for extracts from *The Primary Language Record: Handbook for Teachers* (1988) and *Patterns of Learning* (1990) by M. Barrs, S. Ellis, H. Hester, and A. Thomas.

Deakin University Press for an extract from *The Action Research Planner* (1982) by S. Kemmis and R. McTaggart.

R. Ellis for the use of an unpublished Checklist.

K. Germaine for a table from 'An investigation of leadership traits and skills in relation to microteaching feedback sessions in ELT teaching education', unpublished MA dissertation, Ealing College London (now Polytechnic of West London).

T. Hedge for extracts from *Writing* (1989).

Heinemann Educational Books for extracts from *Evaluating and Selecting EFL Teaching Materials* (1984) by A. Cunningsworth.

L. Lawrence for extracts from 'Language in education: an evaluation of the teaching of structure in Zambian grade 8 classes' (1990). Unpublished PhD thesis.

Macmillan Educational for an extract from *Action Research: Principles and Practice* (1988) by J. McNiff.

H. Miletto for an unpublished Questionnaire and 'Self-evaluation form' used at Ealing College on a Council of Europe course for adult learners.

Multilingual Matters for an extract from 'The need for a multi-perspective approach to the evaluation of foreign language teaching materials' by G. Low (1987), published in *Evaluation and Research in Education: The Durham and Newcastle Research Review*.

NFER-Nelson for the excerpt from *Self-evaluation: A Primary Teacher's Guide* (1988) by J. Moyles.

F. O'Dell and EFL Gazette for a review published in EFL Gazette, February 1990.

Pergamon Press for an extract from 'Evaluation: a way of involving the learner' by M. Oskarsson, cited in J. C. Alderson (ed.): *Evaluation* (1985), Lancaster Practical Papers in English Language Education 6.

The Polytechnic of West London (formerly Ealing College London) for an extract from *The Acquisition of German in a Classroom Context* (1987) by R. Ellis and M. Rathbone.

Prentice Hall International for an extract from *Understanding Language Classrooms* (1989) by D. Nunan.

Pauline Rea-Dickins for extracts from 'Decisions about testing for language teaching purposes' (1989). Keynote address, Japan Association of Language Teachers, University of Tsukuba, Japan.

Research Club in Language Learning for an extract from 'A descriptive model of discourse in the corrective treatment of learners' errors' (1977) by C. Chaudron, published in *Language Learning* 27/1:29–49.

N. Spada for a table from 'Relationships between instructional differences and learning outcomes: a process-product study of communicative language teaching', published in *Applied Linguistics* 8/2:142.

Stirling University Department of Education, for an extract from *The Foreign Language Classroom: An Observational Study* (1981) by R. Mitchell, B. Parkinson, and B. Johnstone.

TOEFL for permission to use the framework from the score comparison table.

TESOL Inc. for a table from 'Differences in the communicative orientation of L2 classrooms' by M. Frölich, N. Spada, and P. Allen, published in *TESOL Quarterly* 19/1:57.

The University of Cambridge Local Examinations Syndicate for the Examiner's assessment form for the RSA Diploma in the Teaching of English as a Foreign Language to Adults, and for extracts from *An Introduction to IELTS*, the *Information Pack: Teachers' Guide* to the Certificate in Communicative Skills in English, and the General Training Module Profile Band Descriptors chart from *IELTS Assessment Guide to the Writing Test*.

M. Williams for an extract from 'A developmental view of classroom observations' (1989) published in *English Language Teaching Journal* 43/2:85–91.